Contracts Companion for Writers is an amazingly comprehensive, easy-to-understand examination of the contracts most important to writers. From publishing and agency contracts to collaboration and work-made-for-hire agreements to permission requests and release forms—all set out in an appendix and on the handy CD-ROM—Tonya Evans-Walls covers everything writers, agents, and other industry professionals need to know about creating and closing deals from a position of knowledge and strength. Of particular value are the key clauses and negotiation points Tonya shares with a professional acumen that only a lawyer experienced in this area can deliver. Her expertise in literary law shines through, and the information provided is invaluable. This book is well written and indispensable for writers of every level. Although the information provided will prove of great worth at any point in your drafting and negotiation process, don't wait until after you've signed on the dotted line to read it, and don't rely on just your agent or attorney to tell you what you need to know. As the cover suggests, put down your pen and open this book first. You'll be glad you did!

—*Dan Poynter*
www.parapublishing.com

Contracts Companion for Writers arrived in my office during the week my agent was negotiating the contract for my second book of creative writing exercises. I immediately opened to the chapter on the publishing agreement and read every single word.

My fear of negotiation and legalese was magically and immediately replaced with confidence and knowledge. *Contracts Companion* is a must-have—a "read it before you think you need it" book for all writers.

—*Bonnie Neubauer*
www.BonnieNeubauer.com
Author, *Write-Brain Workbook: 366 Exercises to Liberate Your Writing* and the forthcoming follow-up of ten hundred ten-minute writing exercises, *Take Ten,* and creator of Story Spinner, a handheld generator of millions of creative writing exercises

Contracts Companion for Writers

Tonya M. Evans-Walls

Legal Write Publications

Philadelphia, Pennsylvania

15 14 13 12 11 10 09 08 07   1 2 3 4 5

ISBN 9780967457987

Publisher's Cataloging-in-Publication
(Provided by Quality Books, Inc.)
        Evans-Walls, Tonya M. (Tonya Marie)
            Contracts companion for writers / Tonya M.
        Evans-Walls.
            p. cm. -- (Literary entrepreneur series)
            Includes index.
            ISBN-13: 9780967457987
            ISBN-10: 096745798X

            1. Authors--Legal status, laws, etc.--United States--
        Popular works. 2. Contracts--United States--Popular
        works. 3. Authors and publishers--United States--
        Popular works.   I. Title. II. Series.

        KF390.A96E924 2007   346.7304'82
                                      QBI07-600119

Request for permissions to reproduce any portion of this book should be addressed to:

Legal Write Publications
ATTN: Permissions Department
P.O. Box 25216
Philadelphia, PA 19119

The Legal Write Publications logo, LE Series™ Books and logo and the title and trade dress of the *Contracts Companion for Writers* are the intellectual property of Legal Write Publications.

Editing by Lisa A. Smith, www.writingandeditingatwork.com

Cover and interior design by Debra Tremper, www.sixpennygraphics.com

To the light of my life and my perfect

provision, my husband,

O. Russel Walls, III

Contents

Symbol Key

When you see this symbol . . .   **It means . . .**

 Myth: Presents, examines, and dispels a common myth.

 Note: Draws your attention to a particular topic of interest.

 Question: Presents and answers a frequently asked question.

 Checklist: Lists several items to consider on a particular topic.

 Legal Note: Examines the facts and disposition of a leading case, or the status of a statute or pending legislation.

 Contract Clause: Presents a key contract clause to be considered.

 Form: Provides the applicable form in Appendix B and on the CD-ROM.

 Illustration or Example: Illustrates a particular issue to clarify an important point.

Preface

This book provides comprehensive coverage of key clauses in many relevant industry contracts, with negotiation points to empower writers in the give-and-take of contract formation and negotiation. It is the third in the Literary Entrepreneur Series™ of legal reference guides for writers and publishing industry professionals. Other books in the series include *Literary Law Guide for Authors: Copyright, Trademark, and Contracts in Plain Language* and *Copyright Companion for Writers*.

In this book, I address the need to reduce to writing important contracts with collaborators and contributors, for example, and to pay attention to the fine print because every word has meaning and is important. I also encourage you to ask questions even (and especially) about boilerplate language of publishing and agency contracts, to recognize and appreciate the key clauses in various contracts, and to negotiate from a position of strength and confidence. Further, I instruct you about what to do when a deal goes badly and how to get your rights back after transferring them. My overall goal is to present essential legal information in a user-friendly way and to help you develop strategies to maximize the value of your artistic and literary creations over the long term—which currently means, in copyright law lingo, the life of the author plus seventy years after the author's death.

All of the contracts I cover are set forth in full in the Forms Appendix and on the CD-ROM included in the back of the book. The information and forms provided should help you to identify issues; formulate questions; better understand common legalese; address and negotiate key points; and empower you to seal deals that honor the blood, sweat, and tears you invested in your work, and the overall value of your work and rights. Nothing in this book, however, should replace competent legal advice from an attorney about your particular legal issues, because every case is different and is based on the individual facts and circumstances of the specific situation.

1 Get It in Writing

From the moment we wake up until the moment we go to sleep, our days are filled with negotiations and agreements—with family (especially kids!), friends, co-workers, employers and employees, salespeople, and even (or particularly) our adversaries. No relationship, whether personal or professional, is immune from this certainty. From politics to pee wee football, our country and, indeed, our world turn on negotiating rights and responsibilities of various parties for innumerable purposes.

We participate in the give-and-take of negotiations basically to get what we want. But negotiations are rarely a zero sum game so, in the famous words of the Rolling Stones, "You can't always get what you want." Therefore, two goals exist in making contracts with others: to maximize what we receive from others and to minimize what we have to give up or do in return. And this reality is certainly present in the world of writing and publishing. But, as you will learn in chapter 2, not all agreements are legally enforceable contracts.

I am often asked (by people who obviously do not watch *People's Court*) whether it is necessary to write down every agreement and sign on the dotted line. The simple answer (which you rarely hear from a lawyer) is no, or at least not necessarily. As you will learn in this book, you need not reduce an agreement to a writing signed by the parties for a legally binding contract to exist, except for agreements required by law to be in writing, like the purchase or sale of real estate or a long-term lease. As long as a verbal agreement contains both the essential and the material elements of a contract (offer, acceptance, consideration, intent to contract, legal capacity to contract, and a legal object of contract, as discussed more fully in chapter 2), that verbal agreement will constitute a binding and legally enforceable agreement, also known as a contract.

Essentially, the term "contract" means a legally enforceable agreement between two competent parties. "Competent" means the contracting parties must be of age and in their right minds. And each party agrees to exchange something of value, like money, for goods or services, for example. Of course, with oral contracts, the hard part is proving the terms if something does not go as planned or if someone fails to perform as expected.

So to be prudent, particularly regarding important agreements you would want to enforce in court or through some other legal proceeding if the other party failed to live up to her end of the bargain, it is best to put your business arrangements in writing because a well-written writing signed by all parties can serve as a clear record of the agreed-upon terms and conditions, and can help to avoid misunderstandings and miscommunications. The absence of a clearly written agreement beforehand is the stuff that protracted litigation, ruined relationships, and whopper legal fees are made of. And it is always amazing how fuzzy someone's memory can be when a deal goes badly and a misunderstanding develops or someone believes she didn't get what she bargained for. This is especially true when the deal involves valuable and unique literary or artistic works and services.

Even if you do not have a formal writing replete with fancy legalese, at a minimum you should send a confirmatory e-mail or letter stating your understanding of the agreement. This will at least memorialize your understanding of your and the other party's rights and responsibilities, and give the other party an opportunity to respond and to clarify potential issues up front, if there is a difference of opinion.

Still Need Convincing?

It is critical to put in writing any business understanding you have with a collaborator (a co-writer or illustrator, for example) or a contributor to your work—anyone who helps to create your book, article, song, and so forth—in order to clarify what rights or permissions are being granted; how expenses, revenues, and copyright are shared (if at all); what happens if someone bails out (or dies) before the work is completed; and what credit is given—just to name a few important factors.

In the case of author and publisher, a signed writing is *essential* because in almost every case copyright is being transferred and therefore copyright law requires it. Additionally, the terms and conditions determine what rights are transferred, what compensation you and the publisher receive, when the rights revert back to you, and what state law governs the contract if a disagreement develops. You should never leave these issues to oral agreements or handshake deals. Always get it in writing, and make sure the contract states clearly what each party agrees to do and what each will receive in return.

As important as it is to reduce these contracts to writing, you must also understand the terms and negotiate—or be certain your representative is negotiating—for the best deal possible. Still, so many creative people shy away from the "negotiations" part, hoping that the terms are reasonable or that their agent or representative will take care of the details. Now hear this, writers: You do a disservice to yourself, given your hard work and considerable talents, when you dot every "i" and cross every "t" in your manuscript but rush through a publishing agreement, often without the guidance of an experienced literary lawyer, and sign it without negotiating the terms from a position of knowledge and strength. Or worse yet, you fail to ensure that all material terms are negotiated favorably and stated clearly in a written agreement signed by you and the agent or publisher.

In the days and weeks leading up to the signing of an agency or publishing agreement, when the agent or publisher has declared interest in your manuscript but you have not yet committed yourself, you are in the strongest position from which to negotiate. And these negotiations are most important because your contract defines what rights you are transferring, what (if any) rights you keep, how your agent and publisher get paid, and how you get paid. Keep in mind that what you agree to today affects you and the other party or parties for years to come. Don't you think that is worth considering seriously and slowly?

Consider this: Although a certain author advance and royalty schedule may seem great now, how fair will it be when you are a best-selling author yet still earning pennies on each book sold while the publisher has long since recouped its investment and is still raking in the lion's share of the profits? Yet this is often what happens when a writer signs a multi-book deal with language like "on the same terms and conditions" in the fine print, language the writer may overlook in her eagerness to reach the amount of the advance or the signature line. Or perhaps transferring all of your rights to a publisher may seem like a good idea now. But what if the publisher does not have any intention of using some of the rights or is actually in no better position than you to properly exploit them? Why transfer them in the first place? This is especially true since it may be more financially beneficial for you to divide the rights and sell them to a number of different buyers then to lump them together and sell to one buyer.

The point is that there is no such thing as a nonnegotiable contract. Do not sign a contract with anyone who tells you there is. Everything is up for discussion (although whether you can secure more favorable terms will depend on your negotiating strength and that of your representative). Compare this process to other areas of your life and ask yourself, "Would I just sign any paper given to me if I were buying a house or car, making a long-term investment, or going into a long-term business relationship with someone I just met?" I venture to guess that your answer to these questions would be no, and that you would take care to read the document and consult with someone more knowledgeable than you to make sure the rights and responsibilities of both parties were set forth clearly and that you were getting not only what is fair but what is in your best interest, to the greatest extent possible.

Although the publishing agreement usually receives a lot of attention, you should be aware, as a Literary Entrepreneur, that other contracts relating to the publishing industry may also be significant for you. In fact, before entering into a publishing agreement with you, a publisher may ask you for copies of a collaboration agreement (if you worked with others to create your book) and a licensing agreement (if you have incorporated the work of others—pictures, illustrations, photographs, and so forth—in your book). In addition, many writers enter into an agency agreement before ever receiving a publishing contract; therefore the agency agreement is also a very important document to become familiar with and to understand.

The Dreaded Fear of Negotiation

The most common fear authors have when faced with a deal is the dreaded fear of negotiation. In the spirit of not wanting to offend, many authors in first-time bargaining situations shy away from asking hard questions and requesting more favorable provisions. Worse still, some authors are intimidated by the process and the documents. That, coupled with an author's excitement over the possibility of any deal, after receiving so many rejections, is a dangerous mix that often spells trouble. Authors do not want to challenge the agent or publisher because they do not want to be perceived as difficult or money hungry. But remember, this is a bottom-line business, and the operative word is "business." Agents and publishers have their own attorneys, and so should you. Any reputable person in the industry understands that offers should be negotiated by competent professionals; it's just business.

2 Contracts Basics

To be legally enforceable, every contract, whether written or oral, must be based on the notion of a bargained exchange that includes three essential elements: offer, acceptance, and legal consideration. In addition to these essential elements, the parties must intend to enter into the contract and to be bound immediately by its terms, also known as a "meeting of the minds." Contracts are governed by state law.

A contract will not be legally enforceable if it is void, such as one that never legally existed because it was for illegal goods or an illegal purpose—or if it is voidable, such as one that exists until canceled by a legally incapacitated party, like a seventeen-year-old recording artist who no longer wants to honor his recording contract. Therefore a contract must also involve (1) legal capacity (the legal power or authority) to enter into the contract in the first place and (2) a legal object or purpose (not one involving illegal drugs or a hit man contracted to murder, for example).

While adults are generally presumed to have capacity, the legal capacity requirement exists to protect certain members of society from being taken advantage of. For example, the law would protect those who are intoxicated or otherwise under the influence, those suffering from a mental impairment, and those who are under age. The law is interested in avoiding potential injustices from occurring where minors or mentally incapacitated persons might agree to terms that the reasonably prudent person would not agree to, given the same facts and circumstances. The law presumes that such parties do not have the ability to appreciate the terms of a contract and therefore do not have a legal intention to enter into contracts.

Offer, Acceptance, and Consideration

A contract is more than an agreement to do or refrain from doing something. It is a legally enforceable agreement between two or more legally competent parties—individuals, businesses, or other organizations—in which one party makes an offer to do or refrain from doing something, the other accepts the offer, and each exchanges something of value, also called consideration. Consideration is a legal concept best described as the benefit or detriment that induces someone to make a promise and enter into a contractual arrangement based on the terms, conditions, rights, and obligations agreed to by the parties involved.

Contracts are legally enforceable only if there is sufficient consideration to show that each party has given something of value to benefit from the deal. For example, if A offers to print B's books for $2,000, and B accepts by giving A $2,000 for the printed books, and A gives B the printed books, each gives something of value.

By contrast, an offer and acceptance without adequate consideration is merely a gift. For instance, if A offers to give B $10, and B accepts but makes no promise in return, then A's transfer of $10 to B is a gift and not a legally enforceable contract. The practical effect is that, generally speaking, B cannot sue A to pay the $10 if A reneges on her promise. But in some cases a court will enforce an agreement made for less than adequate consideration if one party relied to his or her disadvantage on the promise of another. This is known in legalese as promissory estoppel or detrimental reliance.

A contract is void if the promise on which it is based is illegal or illicit. For example, an agreement between two drug dealers about the exchange of money for drugs is not legally enforceable because the promises involve the completion of an illegal act.

Although the actual terms will vary from contract to contract, a valid contract must also contain the material terms—the most important terms—of the agreement: the who, what, where, when, how, and how much of the mutual benefits and obligations. Collectively, these material terms govern the transaction.

If it's not in writing, it's not a legally enforceable contract.

This assumption is false. An oral agreement can be enforceable in court if the basic contract elements exist and the essential terms are mutually agreed upon. But certain contracts are legally required to be in writing. Contracts are governed by state law, which of course differs from state to state. Nonetheless, each state has a Statute of Frauds which requires that certain contracts be in writing. In most cases, the following contracts must be in writing:

- wills
- sale of real property
- lease of property with a term of more than one year

- **contracts with a term of more than one year or a value above a certain amount**
- **assignments of copyright**

Sometimes two people make an oral contract and thereafter one or both of them send a confirming letter, e-mail, or other writing that restates their understanding of the terms and conditions of the contract. It is important to note that any confirming memorandum should express only what was agreed to and not add or exclude any terms already agreed to. You should send such a memorandum immediately, to confirm your understanding and to give the other party a chance to review and clarify her intention in case her understanding is different from yours. This is perfectly legal and certainly preferred to leaving an oral contract to chance.

3 When a Good Deal Goes Bad

When one party fails to perform his or her obligations under the contract, this is known as a breach of the contract, and the non-breaching party may seek to enforce the terms of the contract by any of the various dispute resolution options—negotiation, mediation, arbitration, or litigation—and to collect damages and compel performance or otherwise settle the dispute. The premise of damages is to make the non-breaching party "whole," that is, restored to the position he or she was in before entering into the contract. This premise is different from criminal penalties that seek to punish and to reform behavior.

In most cases, the non-breaching party will receive monetary damages. Sometimes, however, money will not make the non-breaching party whole. For example, when an author licenses her article to a magazine for first serial print publication rights, but the publisher also posts the article on its Web site without obtaining electronic rights, the author may sue for monetary damages. But the author may also not want the article posted online for a variety of reasons. In fact, getting the magazine to remove the article from its Web site may be more valuable to the author than any amount of money she may be entitled to recover. Therefore, the author may, in addition to money damages, demand equitable damages in the form of an injunction to force the magazine publisher to remove the article from the Web site.

The following are the various damages and other remedies available:

❑ Compensatory Damages: Money damages to compensate the non-breaching party for the amount of the loss.

❑ Consequential and Incidental Damages: Additional money damages to compensate the non-breaching party for other costs associated with the breach that could be reasonably anticipated (even if not actually anticipated) by all parties when they entered the contract.

❑ Attorney Fees and Costs: Recovery of the costs of litigation by the non-breaching party if included in the terms of the contract or if otherwise within a judge's discretion to grant.

❑ Liquidated Damages: Monetary damages expressly provided for in the terms of the contract; usually included when actual monetary damages would be difficult to determine if a breach occurred.

❑ Specific Performance: A court order for the breaching party to perform as agreed to in the contract; not applicable to contracts to sing or write, for instance, because this requirement would in effect be indentured servitude (working against one's will); but applicable to contracts involving, for example, the transfer of unique property.

❑ Punitive Damages: Money awarded only in the most egregious contract cases to deter the breaching party and others from repeated occurrences of the wrongdoing; almost never awarded in contract cases.

❑ Rescission: When the contract is terminated and both parties are excused from further performance.

❑ Reformation: When the contract is revised to properly reflect the original intentions of the parties.

Defenses to a Claim of Breach of Contract

Even when breach of contract is established, a defendant may avoid liability by proving at least one of the most common legal defenses:

❑ Lack of Consideration: At least one party did not give something of value to the other party. As a result the transfer is considered a gift instead of a legally enforceable contract.

❑ Duress, Undue Influence, Fraud: One party was under significant pressure (give me your money, or I'll kill you) or was tricked into signing the contract.

❑ Lack of Competence: One of the contracting parties was a minor or was mentally incapable of entering into a legally enforceable contract.

❑ Impossibility: Through no fault of either party, something unforeseeable, such as an act of God, terror, or war, occurred that made it impossible to perform under the terms of the contract.

❏ Illegality: The terms of the contract were illegal, making the contract legally unenforceable.

Alternative Dispute Resolution

Not every dispute needs to wind up in court. In fact, many contract disputes can be settled by effective alternative dispute resolution, also referred to as ADR. ADR seeks to resolve legal controversies outside of a traditional legal forum. The three categories of ADR are negotiation, mediation, and arbitration.

Negotiation usually involves only the parties and, if applicable, their representatives, without a neutral third party to assist in reaching a settlement or to issue a disposition for the case. This should be the first option in every situation, if at all possible. Negotiation is by far the least expensive and least time-consuming option, and it can also be the most gratifying to all because the parties themselves fashion their own mutually agreed to settlement. Any negotiated agreement should, of course, be reduced to writing and signed by the parties. And any settlement that changes the terms or conditions of the original agreement should specifically state the relevant changes and whether the remaining original terms are still effective or whether they are superseded by a new contract. Unfortunately, if the parties reach an impasse in negotiation, the other resolution options become necessary to resolve the conflict.

Mediation is a voluntary process that involves the parties, their representatives (if any), and a neutral third party called (you guessed it) a mediator, selected from a list of mediators. The mediator facilitates communication between the parties and assists them in identifying and clarifying their various interests and in resolving the dispute. The mediator will often suggest a resolution but does not actually impose a binding decision. So the parties are free to accept the mediator's suggestions, to agree to another settlement, or to terminate discussions entirely and seek other alternatives.

Arbitration is basically a hybrid of mediation and litigation. An arbitrator or panel of arbitrators presides over the case the way a judge does in court, and issues a decision referred to as an award. Arbitrations are preferable in many situations, especially those involving smaller amounts of money or highly technical issues like copyright laws, because they tend to be less expensive, quicker, and more flexible than litigation, and the decision often remains private. By contrast, court decisions are generally public record and therefore open to public scrutiny.

The parties can agree to make the arbitrator's decision binding or nonbinding. The determination of whether the award is binding will be set forth in the arbitration clause of a contract, so carefully review any arbitration provision.

This is a typical binding arbitration clause.

Both parties agree that any conflicts regarding the terms and conditions of this contract shall be resolved by binding arbitration in California, according to California law, under the rules and institutional supervision of the American Arbitration Association (AAA). Any decision rendered by the arbitrator may be entered in any court of any country having jurisdiction thereof. The arbitral tribunal shall consist of one neutral arbitrator appointed by the AAA. The arbitrator shall award attorney's fees to the prevailing party.

About the American Arbitration Association

The American Arbitration Association (AAA) is a well-known and widely respected leader in arbitration and mediation services. Additionally, AAA arbitrators are well trained and are generally experts in their respective fields, such as intellectual property matters. It is not uncommon for an arbitration clause in a contract to require the parties to submit to the rules and jurisdiction of the AAA, so you should take the time to learn more about this organization as well as local arbitration tribunals. For more information about the services offered by the AAA, visit www.adr.org.

4 Transferring Your Rights and Getting Them Back

Any contracts you enter into regarding your literary or artistic works will likely involve intellectual property rights. Intellectual property is essentially personal property created with the mind and evidenced in some tangible form. What you don't know about intellectual property ownership can jeopardize your rights and potentially expose you to legal liability. So below is a crash course in the differences between the various types of intellectual property and a brief discussion of copyright.

Property Created with the Mind

Intellectual property has been defined generally as "creations of the mind" that are afforded the status of property and thus have value that is capable of protection. Intellectual property is governed by various national and international laws, and generally gives its owner the exclusive right to do or authorize certain things regarding the property. The three basic types of intellectual property are copyrights, trademarks or service marks, and patents.

Copyright: A copyright protects an author's original artistic or literary work, whether published or unpublished. Under copyright law, the term "author" has a special meaning: the creator of an original literary or artistic work. Thus, the term applies not only to writers but to photographers, singers, painters, sculptors—anyone who creates a literary or artistic work. Examples of literary and artistic works include manuscripts, book covers, song lyrics, sheet music, musical scores, paintings, sketches, sound recordings (music), films, and photographs. And those lists are not all-inclusive.

Trademark: A trademark protects a word, phrase, symbol, or device—the mark—used in business (referred to in the law as commerce) to identify and distinguish one product from another. For example, Jump at the Sun® is a registered trademark for children's fiction and nonfiction books about history, sports, the arts, spirituality, musicians, biography, friendship, family, poetry, and school.

Service Mark: A service mark protects a word, phrase, symbol, or device—again, the mark—used in business to identify and distinguish one service from another. For example, Lightning Source® is a registered service mark for wholesale distributorship services in the field of on-demand printing and electronic media.

Patent: The patent is probably the least used intellectual property in the publishing industry. A patent protects an invention by granting the inventor the right to exclude others from producing or using the inventor's discovery or invention for a specific time. Some examples of patentable inventions are the talking book, an e-book reader, a typewriter, and an Internet-based system and method for highlighting search results such as that used by Google. Not all intellectual property lawyers practice patent law because a patent practice requires that attorneys have a science degree and take an additional bar examination; patent attorneys usually have some background in technology or engineering.

A Crash Course in Copyright

No one word is more misused or more misunderstood by writers than the word "copyright." This single word creates such confusion and lends itself to so much misinformation because rumors, assumptions, and complicated changes in the law make it difficult for writers to separate fact from fiction. But because copyright consists of such a valuable bundle of rights, it is imperative that writers fully comprehend the nature of copyright and the process by which it is protected. The following is a general overview of copyright to help you appreciate the nature of the rights involved in the various contracts discussed in this book. For a complete discussion of copyright, see my books *Copyright Companion for Writers* and *Literary Law Guide for Authors: Copyright, Trademark, and Contracts in Plain Language.*

The federal Copyright Act provides copyright protection to "authors" (creators) of "original works." The act covers literary, musical, artistic, dramatic, choreographic, pictorial, sculptural, and audiovisual works, and certain other creative works of an intellectual nature. Copyright protection is available for both published works (those made available to the public) and unpublished works (those shared with only a few or not at all).

Copyright exists *automatically* when a work is created. For the purposes of copyright law, a work is created when it is fixed in a copy or phonorecord for the first time. By "copy" the law means material objects—such as books, manuscripts, electronic files, Web sites, e-mail, sheet music, musical scores, film, videotape, or microfilm—from which a work can be read or visually perceived either directly or with the aid of a machine or device. Phonorecords are material objects such as cassette tapes, CDs, or LPs. Thus, for example, a song (the work) can be fixed in sheet music (copies) or on a CD (phonorecord) or both. If a work is created over time, the copyright applies automatically to whatever part is fixed on a particular date. So as soon as you write the first two paragraphs of your book, whether by hand on paper or by keying them into a computer, those paragraphs are immediately and automatically copyrighted—even if you don't get around to writing the third paragraph until a week or a year later.

In general, the Copyright Act gives a copyright owner the exclusive right to do and to authorize others to do (or preclude others from doing) the following:

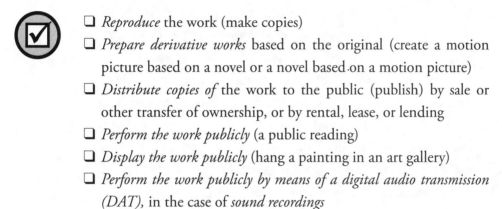

- ❑ *Reproduce* the work (make copies)
- ❑ *Prepare derivative works* based on the original (create a motion picture based on a novel or a novel based on a motion picture)
- ❑ *Distribute copies of* the work to the public (publish) by sale or other transfer of ownership, or by rental, lease, or lending
- ❑ *Perform the work publicly* (a public reading)
- ❑ *Display the work publicly* (hang a painting in an art gallery)
- ❑ *Perform the work publicly by means of a digital audio transmission (DAT),* in the case of *sound recordings*

Collectively, these rights are often referred to as an author's exclusive bundle of rights.

Copyright Creation Versus Protection

If you have created an original work in some tangible form—in writing or on film or tape or canvas, for example—then you don't have to do anything. You automatically own a copyright in your work. To demonstrate to the world that you own your work, you should use a copyright notice (although you are not required by law to use the notice). The notice should contain the copyright symbol (©) or the word Copyright (or its abbreviation Copr.), the date, and the copyright owner's name.

But you should register your copyright for further protection. Registration creates a public record of the facts and circumstances pertaining to the copyright. While registration is *not* necessary for your copyright to exist, the Copyright Act gives you certain advantages under the law if you do register your work.

For example:

- ❏ You can file an infringement suit only after your copyright is registered.
- ❏ If registered before or within five years of publication, registration establishes sufficient (*prima facie*) evidence in court of the validity of the copyright and of the facts stated in the registration certificate.
- ❏ If you register within three months after publication of the work or prior to an infringement, the defendant is required to prove that infringement does not exist. This is a critical advantage because ordinarily the person who files a lawsuit has to prove his or her case; but if you have registered your copyright in a timely manner, then the burden of proof falls to the defendant.
- ❏ If registration is made within three months after publication of the work or prior to an infringement, statutory damages and attorney's fees will be available to the copyright owner in court actions, in the judge's discretion. Otherwise, only an award of actual damages and profits is available.
- ❏ Registration allows the copyright owner to record the registration with the U.S. Customs Service for protection against the importation of infringing copies.

How Copyrights Are Transferred

Any or all of the copyright owner's bundle of rights or any subdivision of those rights may be transferred to a third party. In other words, you may transfer one right in the bundle to one person or entity and another right or two or three to another person or entity. A transfer is defined in section 101 of the Copyright Act as an "assignment, mortgage, grant of an exclusive license, transfer by will or intestate succession, or any other change in the ownership of any or all of the exclusive rights in a copyright whether or not it is limited in time or place of effect."

Generally, there are three types of transfers: (1) a nonexclusive license, under which you remain the owner of your work and give the licensee permission to use your work without the right to exclude others from doing so; (2) an exclusive license, under which you remain the owner of your work but no one other than the licensee has permission to use the work—in many cases not even you; and (3) an assignment, under which you give ownership of your work to the transferee. Further limits on transfer include the actual rights transferred, the term, and the geographical scope. To be valid, the transfer of exclusive rights must be in a written agreement signed by the owner of the rights conveyed (or the owner's authorized agent). But a nonexclusive license does not require a written agreement. So, for example, the transfer of the exclusive right of publication to a publisher or agent requires a signed agreement, but the nonexclusive permission to reproduce an excerpt of a literary work in a newsletter does not.

As a matter of course, however, you should get all agreements relating to your copyright interests in writing. Having a signed agreement memorializes the terms and reduces the likelihood of misunderstandings as to what was promised by each party.

A copyright may also be transferred by operation of law. For instance, copyright can be bequeathed by will or by state law if a person dies without a will. Copyright is a personal property right, and it is subject to the various state laws and regulations that govern the ownership, inheritance, or transfer of personal property and the terms of contracts or conduct of business. For information about relevant state laws, consult an attorney in your area.

Copyright assignments can be filed, or recorded, in the Copyright Office as transfers of copyright ownership. Recording the assignment gives notice to the world that the copyright interest has been transferred. Although you are not required to record the transfer to make it valid, recording the assignment does provide certain legal advantages and may be required to validate the transfer against third parties. For instance, under certain conditions, recordation establishes the order of priority between conflicting transfers (that is, who received the transfer first), or between a conflicting transfer and a nonexclusive license. Recordation also establishes a public record of the transaction and provides "constructive notice," which is a legal term meaning that members of the public are deemed to have been notified even if they have not actually received notice of the transfer. To establish constructive notice, the recorded document must describe the work with specificity so that it can be identified by a reasonable search, and the work must be registered with the Copyright Office.

Reclaiming Your Copyright after Transfer

Did you know that regardless of the terms of your transfer document (e.g., a publishing agreement or a license), you have the right to reclaim your copyright? Discussion about this little-known legal right for authors is just starting to emerge in the publishing industry. Publishers, for instance, may not want authors to know that the "life of copyright" term in most publishing agreements can be rendered null and void if a statutory termination is properly effected. But because different versions of the copyright law apply to different works, depending on when they were created, registered, and transferred, and depending on who transferred the rights, there are different rules for terminating transfers of those works to third parties. I will examine pre-1978 transfers and those transfers made on or after January 1, 1978; but if you have a specific question regarding a potential transfer termination, please contact an intellectual property attorney who is well versed in literary law and transfer termination issues.

Pre-1978 Transfers

Due to several amendments to copyright law, pre-1978 works, governed by the Copyright Act of 1909, can be protected for up to ninety-five years. This includes the initial twenty-eight-year term of copyright (the initial term), plus the first twenty-eight-year renewal term (renewal term), plus an additional nineteen-year term (bonus term), and, thanks to Sonny Bono, the extended twenty-year term (extended bonus term). Through this series of statutory revisions, pre-1978 works enjoy an additional sixty-seven years beyond the initial term of protection (provided the renewal was either affirmatively or automatically renewed).

But transfer rules do not hinge on the date of creation or registration per se but on the date the copyright was transferred. Section 304(c) of the Copyright Act allows a writer to reclaim his or her copyright if those rights were transferred (either by the writer or his or her heirs) before January 1, 1978. The window of opportunity to begin the transfer termination process begins either fifty-six years after the date the copyright was originally secured or on January 1, 1978, whichever is later. For pre-1978 transfers, writers actually have two opportunities to reclaim copyright; if the first opportunity, fifty-six years after transfer, passes, the second and final opportunity to recapture the last twenty years of copyright protection occurs seventy-five years after transfer. You must give at least two years but not more than ten years notice to the transferee that you intend to terminate the copyright transfer.

Post-1977 Transfers

Creators of works transferred on or after January 1, 1978, enjoy similar but not identical transfer termination rules. Section 203 of the Copyright Act provides that a transfer or license of copyright (or any right in the bundle of rights) executed by the author (but unlike a pre-1978 transfer *not* a transfer made by anyone other than the author) on or after January 1, 1978, is subject to termination under the following conditions:

❑ A single author who executed a grant may terminate it. If the author is deceased, then whoever is entitled to exercise more than one-half of that author's rights may terminate it.

❏ If two or more authors executed a grant of a joint work, a majority of the authors who executed it may terminate it. If any of the joint authors is dead, his or her termination interest may be exercised by whoever is entitled to exercise more than one-half of that author's interest.

This single, extremely valuable section of the Copyright Act, allowing for the reclaiming of rights by terminating transfers, empowers authors.

Note that the statutory termination provision does not apply to works made for hire or to transfers made by will. The termination right also does not apply to rights arising under foreign laws or derivative works. In the case of derivative works (for example, a movie based on a book), termination of the rights to the underlying work (the book) does not prevent the continued display and distribution of the derivative movie. Once the rights are terminated, however, no new derivative works can be created without permission of the author.

Not surprisingly, the rules to exercise the statutory termination right are specific and must be strictly adhered to or the right will be forever lost. In addition, the Copyright Office does not provide printed forms for the use of persons serving notices of termination.

The specific rules are as follows. First, termination can be effected only during a five-year window of opportunity. For works transferred on or after January 1, 1978, the window begins thirty-five years after the grant was made. Special rules apply if the right transferred is the right of publication. In that case, the window begins thirty-five years from the date of publication or at the end of forty years from the date the transfer was executed, whichever is earlier. Presumably this modification accounts for the gap in time between the date a publishing agreement is signed and the date the work is actually published.

Second, the original owner must deliver to the grantee a signed, written, advance termination notice, which includes the effective date of termination, not less than two years or more than ten years before the termination is to take effect. The notice must be signed by the original owner (or owners, as per the statute) or a duly authorized agent, who may be an attorney-in-fact under a power of attorney, or, if the original owner is deceased, an heir or beneficiary under a will. The notice must be recorded with the Copyright Office *before* the termination is to take place, and, of course, the underlying work must be registered with the Copyright Office.

Third, the Copyright Act states, "Termination of the grant may be effected *notwithstanding any agreement to the contrary . . .*" Therefore, you cannot "contract around" this right. In other words, you cannot waive these rights by contract. Your right to terminate exists until it is exercised or lost, pursuant to the terms of the statute.

Let's bring this topic home by way of example. Assume that Author, at age 30, signs a publishing agreement with XYZ Publisher on January 1, 2003. In that agreement, Author transfers to XYZ the right to publish in hardback and paperback and all subsidiary rights. The work is published eighteen months later, on July 1, 2004. On January 1, 2010, XYZ licenses the right to develop a motion picture based on the book.

Because the transferring contract was signed on January, 1, 2003, before the publication date, the five-year window springs into effect thirty-five years later, on January, 1, 2038, and ends on January 1, 2043. During that window, Author has the right to terminate the agreement and reclaim all rights transferred to Publisher. If Author intends to terminate the publishing agreement on the first date the window comes into effect, she will have to send a termination notice to Publisher or his assignee no earlier than January 1, 2028, and no later than January 1, 2036. Once the transfer terminates, Publisher can no longer create any derivative works or license that right to others.

It is crucial to understand when the termination window exists and to plan properly to reclaim your rights. Additionally, you should plan for the reclamation of your rights in your will so that your family, executor, or trustee knows that your intellectual property exists, and understands how to manage and protect those rights after your death. This, of course, means that you must consult a trust and estates attorney, one who is familiar with intellectual property laws, to create an estate plan that includes a will and perhaps a trust, financial power of attorney, and healthcare power of attorney with a medical directive (aka a living will), so that you protect not only your tangible personal property and real estate but also your intellectual property. In particular, consider creating a testamentary trust in your will to name a literary trustee knowledgeable about intellectual property, to maintain and administer your intellectual property rights after your death. This is a special type of trustee who will probably be someone other than a person you would usually name, because the literary trustee should be familiar with intellectual property law.

5 What Freelancers Need to Know

Submitting articles, essays, poems, photographs, songs, or other literary and artistic works to a collective work such as a magazine, newspaper, anthology, or Web site involves rights in the individual contribution owned by the contributor and in the final collective work owned by the publisher. So freelancers should understand the nature of their rights *before* submitting their work—not after.

Copyright in your literary or artistic contribution to a collective work is completely separate and distinct from copyright in the collective work as a whole, and vests initially in you as the author of the contribution. And unless you expressly assign your individual rights in your work to the copyright owner of the collective work, that person or company is presumed to have acquired only a license to reproduce and distribute your contribution as part of that particular collective work, as well as any revision of that collective work, and any later collective work in the same series. For example, if you submit an article for publication in a printed magazine, unless you agree to some other arrangement, the magazine's publisher by default only has a license to include your work (the individual contribution) in the magazine (the collective work) in print. I refer to the printed magazine because an additional license is generally required to publish in other forms, such as electronically.

Of course, if you sign a contract that requires you to transfer some or all of your rights in your individual work to the publisher of the collective work, you should pay particular attention to whether the transfer is so comprehensive that it prevents even you from using your work for a certain time or forever. And you should be compensated handsomely for this exchange. Additionally, you should confirm whether the publisher seeks to publish in print, electronically, or both, or by some other means.

If you've read this book from the beginning, you know I recommend that you have a formal written agreement that describes your arrangement with the publisher. But even a series of e-mails confirming the various terms and conditions is sufficient. Whatever the method of memorializing the deal, it should be clear whether the publisher is acquiring first serial rights, second serial rights (also known as reprint rights), all rights, or whether the publisher has commissioned you to create a work as a work-made-for- hire to be used in a collective work. The following chart will help you to distinguish between these various rights:

First serial rights	The publisher acquires the right to publish your unpublished work before anyone else does. Consider limiting this transfer by indicating a particular territory (North America) and language (English). Note: In publishing contracts, the term "North America" may have a specific meaning that differs from what you learned in geography class. In the contracts, sometimes "North America" includes Canada and sometimes it doesn't, so be sure to confirm whether the publisher intends to include Canada.
Second serial rights (aka reprint rights)	The publisher acquires the right to publish your work after the first serial publication. You are usually required to note where the work was originally published.
Work made for hire	This means that the publisher—not you, the writer—owns the copyright. Try to avoid this if possible unless you receive adequate financial compensation. Work-made-for-hire arrangements must be agreed to *before* you begin working, even if the actual agreement is reduced to writing at a later date, or else they are generally not valid because copyright comes into existence as soon as an original literary or artistic work is fixed in a tangible form and is therefore capable of being copied. See chapter 9 for additional information about work-made-for-hire agreements.
One-time rights	Sometimes a newspaper editor seeks one-time rights, meaning the right to publish your article once, regardless of whether that newspaper is first or second in line to publish.

Clauses to Consider

If you are presented with a typical publishing agreement for individual contributions to a collective work such as a magazine, you will likely see the following clauses in the contract.

Introductory/Recitals Paragraph: The beginning paragraph in all contracts generally identifies the parties to the contract, their legal status (individual or company, for example), and their place of residence or principal place of business. This paragraph may also identify the date the contract becomes effective. This date can refer retroactively to a prior date.

Services: This clause describes the services or work product the freelancer will provide. For example, it may state whether the freelancer is expected to submit only one submission, multiple submissions at the same time, or perhaps multiple submissions over time. This paragraph should also state the genre or topic of the submission, the required form it should take, the preferred manner of submission (electronic via e-mail or on CD-ROM or hard copy), and the word or page count, if applicable.

Rights: The rights paragraph sets forth the rights being granted or licensed to the publisher. If you do not intend to transfer copyright ownership in your work to the publisher, the contract should clearly state that you are only licensing permission to the publisher to use your work in a certain way for a certain purpose and a certain amount of time, and that you reserve any and all rights not expressly mentioned. If, however, you do intend to grant copyright to the publisher, you should receive a fee that properly reflects such a substantial transfer of rights. Be aware that most publishers have their own legal departments to draft their "standard" agreement, solely with the publisher's rights in mind. And that standard contract just might take the kitchen-sink mentality and transfer every conceivable right to the publisher. So let the writer beware.

Payments: A paragraph in the contract should address how, when, and how much you will get paid and whether you'll have to return any payments if the deal goes south for any number of reasons. Remember that when you get paid is as important if not more important than how much, particularly if you write articles for publications that pay small sums of money. You want to receive your money as quickly as possible, so push for "on acceptance" rather than "on publication," because publication dates can be months after acceptance. At a minimum, try to receive some portion of your payment on acceptance and the remainder on publication, and log anticipated pay dates so you can keep track of the money that's due to you from various publishers.

Finally, try to get a "kill fee" provision in your contract if you have been asked to write an article or shoot a pictorial (as opposed to submitting something you've already written or created). A kill fee simply provides that you will be paid a certain amount of money if the publisher decides, for whatever reason, not to publish your work (i.e., kill it) after the work has already been created or accepted. The amount of the kill fee can vary widely, but it is generally quoted as a percentage (10 percent, 25 percent, 50 percent, and so forth) of the total original payment.

6 CYA: Media Perils Insurance

Media perils insurance generally protects writers, publishers, and other providers of media content in case they are sued for copyright and trademark infringement, idea misappropriation and right of publicity claims, defamation (both libel and slander), or invasion of privacy claims. Regular general liability policies that cover bodily injury and property damage caused by a company and its employees do not generally cover media perils. So if you need this protection, you will have to add a media perils rider to your general business liability policy or secure a separate policy specifically to cover these potential liabilities.

Not all writers need media perils insurance. For example, it may not be necessary or cost effective for a fiction writer to get a media perils insurance policy since the odds are, assuming the writer has not infringed, that such a writer will not be sued for violation of any of the media perils causes of action. But all writers who self-publish stories about real people and experiences, all non-fiction writers who are not covered as an additional insured by their publishers, and all publishers (regardless of genre) should seriously consider purchasing a media perils policy because ultimately the publisher will be responsible for the content it publishes. And even when a writer represents and warrants that his or her work is original and does not violate or infringe anyone else's rights, an indemnification provision is of little value if the writer has no money to defend a suit or actually indemnify the publisher, and the publisher has the deep pockets media perils plaintiffs salivate over when filing a lawsuit.

One Size Does Not Fit All

Two basic types of media perils coverage generally exist: claims made and occurrence. The former is the more affordable, although that statement is relative because premiums are pricey and usually start at a cost of several thousand dollars. Claims-made policies cover claims made during the term of the policy but not claims made after the policy has expired.

Occurrence coverage is more comprehensive and covers claims relating to any work published during the term of the policy, even after the policy expires. Of course, this type of coverage is also significantly more costly.

As with any type of insurance, premiums can be managed by increasing or decreasing your deductible. Other considerations will also affect the cost of premiums: costs of defense (meaning whether attorneys' fees are included in the coverage limit or whether they are an additional expense); extent of coverage; whether legal opinions from the insured's attorney are required; coverage of Internet activities like blogging and podcasting; and the territory covered by the policy (United States versus worldwide). Of course this list is not all-inclusive. In fact, a review of only a few policies and provider Web sites proves the list of variables to consider is extensive and exhaustive. But these are some of the more important items to assess when considering and comparing media perils policies.

Some organizations, like PMA, the Independent Book Publishers Association (formerly Publisher's Marketing Association), provide coverage to their members at a significant savings. So you should check with your writer's organization to see if such a member benefit exists.

Author as an Additional Insured

All mainstream publishers and many independent publishers carry media perils insurance to protect themselves against claims for infringement and the like. But unless a writer is added to the policy as an additional insured, the writer is on her own in case of a lawsuit. What makes matters worse for writers is that the publishing agreement usually requires the writer to provide a warranty that the work is original and does not infringe on anyone's rights, and to agree to indemnify the publisher if it turns out that the work was not original. This means that if the suit is lost, the writer will be on the hook financially not only for the award to the plaintiff but also for her legal fees and costs and those of the publisher as well.

Of course, this seems fair in some respects because only the writer really knows if she copied someone else's work. But in the case of other media perils causes of action, like right of privacy, right of publicity, and defamation, the line may not be so bright. So writers should request, in the publishing agreement, that they be added to a publisher's policy as an additional insured. This is a negotiation term that may not be in the original standard form, but it can certainly be added if you ask.

7 The Players and the Process

The process of literary property acquisitions involves a number of professionals. This chapter identifies and explains the roles of the various parties and describes the acquisitions process itself.

The Agent

It is common to hear writers lament, regardless of their level within the industry, that it is more difficult to land an agent than it is to find a publisher willing to publish their books. There is some truth to this. Although writers do not need agents in all situations, they do need an agent when a publisher reviews manuscripts by invitation only or accepts manuscripts only from a literary agent or lawyer. So sending unagented, unsolicited manuscripts to publishers is pure folly in most cases. It's folly because publishers seek to communicate only with professionals they have relationships with, those who know the business and have demonstrated they can present literary properties with potential financial viability.

Great agents and agencies are in high demand because they have demonstrated success in providing *the* critical service in the literary representation process—access to decision makers—and parlaying that access into actual placement, also known as the sale. If you are in search of an agent, word of mouth and referrals are tried-and-true methods of landing the right one. Also, review the acknowledgement pages of books like yours or consult trade publications like the *Writer's Digest.* Another option is to check out books like *Writer's Market* and *Literary Marketplace,* and Web sites like www. publishersmarketplace.com.

But as with most things, one size does not fit all in the world of literary agencies. So finding the right agent is key. That does not necessarily mean the most prestigious one or the one with an office near you. It means you must identify agents who specialize in your particular genre of writing.

A good literary agent generally does the following:

❑ Enters into a written agreement with the writer.

❑ Acts primarily as an intermediary between writer and editor to identify the writer's genre and target market and to query or submit the manuscript to a list of publishing houses that cater to that particular genre and market.

❑ Constantly cultivates relationships within the industry to increase potential opportunities for her clients.

❑ Knows and successfully negotiates the basic deal points.

❑ Receives a writer's compensation, deducts his or her commission, and then pays the writer in a timely fashion.

❑ Provides editorial guidance and light editing for the writer during the writing process.

❑ Keeps the writer reasonably informed of submissions and responses.

A good literary agent generally *does not* do the following:

❑ Charge a fee up front (i.e., a reading fee). An agent's compensation comes in the form of a commission (usually 10 to 20 percent) if and when she sells a property. This caveat does not include extraordinary expenses (e.g., Fed Ex vs. regular USPS postage, travel, and the like). But these costs should be reasonable and documented; and after a certain dollar amount they should be preapproved by the writer. You should also consider a cap on costs, above which the agent must get authorization to incur charges.

❑ Name-drop clients and recent sales unless already public knowledge or with the consent of the clients.

❑ Offer his or her own fee-based editorial services or strongly recommend one editorial company in particular.

Because of the importance of the literary agent and the challenge in finding just the right fit, you will likely have to submit query letters to a number of agents before landing one willing to take you on.

The Literary Lawyer

A literary lawyer can serve as an agent to sell literary properties, as noted above. Another role of the literary lawyer is more limited, but often very valuable—that of a professional independent party to review the contract and advise the writer about the terms of the deal. In this capacity, the literary lawyer identifies what additional terms, if any, should be included and what terms should be revised or deleted. This role is complementary to the agent's role in "getting" the deal or is the key negotiation role when an author does not have an agent (e.g., in a sale to an independent publishing house). The value of a literary lawyer to a writer is that the writer receives an independent legal opinion from someone knowledgeable about publishing contracts (not all agents are lawyers); someone who, in most cases, is working for an hourly rate rather than for a percentage or commission and therefore, in theory, is not biased by the hopes of a piece of the deal or the author's career. Further, some agents (consciously or subconsciously) do not want to upset their existing relationships within the industry and therefore do not push for every last deal point that might benefit a writer.

Literary lawyers can also vet manuscripts for potential legal issues; assist in securing permissions or registering, licensing, and reclaiming your intellectual property rights; and prepare and negotiate other legal agreements you may enter into as a result of your manuscript, such as a licensing or collaboration agreement.

Lastly, literary lawyers can represent publishers and draft and negotiate a company's standard contract with authors.

A good literary lawyer generally does the following:

- ❑ Reviews contracts and advises the writer on the terms.
- ❑ Negotiates additional terms with the publisher, if appropriate.
- ❑ Works actively with the existing professionals (agent, publicist, editor, contracts department) to understand the status of the deal, explain the terms and status to you, and add to rather than detract from the process.
- ❑ Stays on top of current trends and deals in the industry.
- ❑ Vigorously negotiates on behalf of the writer.
- ❑ Maintains the ethical duties to the client of confidentiality and loyalty, thus at all times putting the best interests of the client ahead of his or her own.
- ❑ Assists the writer in acquiring any necessary permissions to use third-party copyrighted materials and releases from interviewees and the like.
- ❑ Drafts publishing, agency, collaboration, work-made-for-hire, options, licenses, and other contracts within the industry.

❏ Vets manuscripts for potential legal issues and advises clients about how to avoid or minimize potential liability.

A good literary lawyer generally *does not* do the following:

❏ Steal a deal away from an agent who placed the work.

❏ Blur the line between lawyer and agent. As noted above, all lawyers owe a professional duty of loyalty and confidentiality to the client, but an agent has only a fiduciary and contractual relationship with the client. Of course, ethical cannons may forbid a lawyer from participating financially in the outcome of a client's legal matter or at least substantially regulate a lawyer who has a fiduciary relationship with, and financial interest in, a client.

The Editor

There are several types of editors in the publishing industry. For purposes of this discussion, "editor" refers to a decision maker employed by a publishing company to seek, review, and purchase manuscripts (or authors to create manuscripts) on behalf of the publisher. This process is known as acquisitions. The acquisitions editor (AE) may also facilitate the final editing process, and oversee the layout, design, production, and marketing of the book.

The AE relies on queries, proposals, and existing relationships with writers, agents, and others within the industry to learn about new properties and story ideas that might match the publisher's various book programs.

Once the AE identifies a potential purchase, he or she reviews the manuscript, evaluates the author's writing abilities, identifies the potential market and market penetration, and considers an appropriate publication schedule. The AE also pitches the manuscript internally to some or all of the editorial, marketing, sales, and upper management personnel within the company to evaluate the financial and overall merits of acquiring the manuscript. Finally, the AE is responsible for negotiating the contractual terms of the publishing agreement with the author or author's representative and overseeing the publication process (sometimes at the macro level and sometimes at the hands-on level of a development or production editor).

A good acquisitions editor generally does the following:

❏ Maintains a broad range of relationships with authors, author representatives, and industry professionals.

- ❑ Plans the best possible market penetration for the book.
- ❑ Knows his or her company's publishing needs and schedule.
- ❑ Knows the company's standard contract terms.
- ❑ Facilitates a smooth, orderly, and efficient contract negotiation.
- ❑ Understands all aspects of the prepress, marketing, and publication processes.
- ❑ Facilitates the polishing of the manuscript and provides support to the author.

A good acquisitions editor generally *does not* do the following:

- ❑ Fail to give the author a workable publication schedule.
- ❑ Promise terms that are conveniently left out of the term sheet or contract.
- ❑ Discourage an author from consulting with an agent or lawyer.
- ❑ Fail to keep the author informed of changes to the manuscript or publication schedule and process.

The Process of Acquisitions

After completing your manuscript, do your homework to research potential literary agents and publishers. The next step is to narrow your focus to those agents who represent work like yours, and query them according to their submission guidelines. A word to the wise: don't get fancy or think outside the box at this point. Follow the agent's instructions and make it easy for the agent to say yes. Agents are well-meaning but busy people. And one way to quickly end up in an agent's circular file (also known as the trash can) is to submit a query or, worse yet, an entire manuscript in a form and manner not accepted by the agent.

Once you have secured an agent (and, of course, have entered into a written agency agreement like the one referred to in chapter 10 and Appendix B), the agent does his or her own research and pitches your work on your behalf to editors who may be interested and receptive. If they bite, the agent submits your work to the publisher or publishers who have expressed interest. If submitted to more than one publisher, the agent will note in the cover letter that the submission is a "simultaneous submission." When the publishing house receives it, the editor must "fall in love with the project" (anyone who has received a letter from an editor will chuckle or cry after reading that phrase) in order to strongly advocate for the manuscript when he or she presents it to other editors, the marketing department, and others at the publishing house.

Assuming the editor convinces the internal decision makers to give the project a green light, the editor often presents a term sheet that sets forth the basic terms offered. This is a good time for the writer to secure a literary lawyer because after the material terms are agreed to, the editor or the company's legal department sends its standard contract for review and comment (or, they hope, a signature). Negotiations continue, revisions to the contract are discussed, and, if agreed upon, made. And then the long-awaited moment arrives—the writer signs on the dotted line.

8 The Collaboration Agreement

Although the writer's life is often solitary, sometimes two or more people decide to contribute to one work. This situation can be a blessing or a curse, depending on how you set up your professional relationship with your collaborators. If you intend to work with someone else to create a joint work, you should consider entering into a collaboration agreement.

A collaboration agreement is used when two or more people contribute to a book; the contributors may be, for example, two authors or an author and an illustrator. The collaboration agreement sets forth the understanding between the parties regarding the nature of the work, their business relationship, what they will each contribute, what percentage of revenue for the book each will receive, and so forth.

Clauses to Consider

Description of the Work: As with other contracts discussed in this book, the paragraph used to describe the work is of paramount importance if the work has not yet been created. You want to draft this paragraph to address the genre and the number of words or pages, and you may want to include chapter summaries or an outline as an exhibit, to avoid unnecessary conflict about the work to be created.

No Agency: The contract should expressly state that the collaborators are separate legal entities, unless a different arrangement is contemplated.

No Agency: The parties to this Agreement are independent of one another, and nothing contained in this Agreement shall make a partnership, agency, or joint venture between them.

Collaboration. This paragraph actually describes the nature of the collaboration and the responsibilities of each party. Additionally, it addresses what happens if someone cannot complete his or her work because of withdrawal from the collaboration for various reasons, including sickness and death. It could also include the definite dates by which each collaborator must complete his or her portion of the work.

Collaboration. Each party agrees to cooperate with the other as joint authors of the Work, to share equally in all tasks and responsibilities as may be necessary to complete the Work, and to do what is necessary to secure its publication and other exploitation. To clarify the respective duties of each party, the responsibilities shall be divided as follows:

(a) Collaborator 1 shall be primarily responsible for

_____.

(b) Collaborator 2 shall be primarily responsible for

_____.

(c) This Agreement shall remain in effect for the duration of the Term (unless otherwise terminated before such time), and shall be binding upon each party's heirs and successors. In the event of the death or disability (either mental or physical) of either party that will prevent completion of his or her respective portion of the Work, the other party shall have the right to complete that portion or to hire a third party to complete that portion and shall adjust the authorship credit to reflect the revised authorship arrangements. The deceased or disabled party shall receive payments pursuant to Paragraph __ pro rata to the proportion of his or her work completed or, in the case of a revision or sequel, shall receive payments pursuant to Paragraph __ after deduction for the cost of revising or creating the sequel with respect to his or her portion of the Work. In that case, the active party shall have the sole power to license and contract with respect to the Work, and approval of the personal representative, heirs, or conservator of the deceased or disabled party shall not be required. If all parties are deceased, the respective heirs or personal representatives shall take the place of the parties for all purposes.

Division of Income and Expenses: The terms of a collaboration agreement should specifically outline how income and expenses are shared. The following clause is a default fifty-fifty split for both income and expenses; the actual division should be negotiated on a case-by-case basis, depending on the effort and value of contributions of the various collaborators.

 Division of Income and Expenses: Income and expenses generated by or on behalf of the Work shall be divided as follows:

Division of Income. Net Income, defined as gross income as reduced by reasonable expenses, shall be divided equally between the parties and paid directly to each party (or her designee as designated in writing). If either party receives income payable to the other party, the receiving party shall give notice to the other party and make immediate payment to the other party of such amounts as are due hereunder.

Division of Expenses. Expenses to produce the Work shall be divided equally between the parties. Each party shall provide written proof of expenses and maintain a proper accounting of such expenses and corresponding payments. Unless otherwise provided, the parties' expenses shall be reimbursed from the first proceeds received, including but not limited to advances.

Creative and Business Decisions: The contract should also address how creative and business decisions will be made and who, if anyone, will have the final say in case of a disagreement.

Copyright, Trademarks, and Other Proprietary Rights: The contract should discuss how copyright ownership is shared. By default, the copyright in joint works is owned equally by each collaborator. This is true regardless of how much each party contributes to the joint work. So if you intend a different split in copyright ownership, you must specify the actual division. Keep in mind that a discussion of how income is shared is completely separate from actual copyright ownership. For example, a collaborator could have a 50 percent interest in any income but not own any share of the copyright. So carefully consider this issue with an experienced lawyer.

Authorship Credit: Credits should be clearly set forth in the contract. Some contracts specify the size of font and, in the case of famous authors writing with less well-known authors, the credit sometimes reads "Suzie Star _with_ Patsi Pen" instead of "Suzie Star _and_ Patsi Pen." When a ghostwriter is used, the actual author receives no credit and generally enters into a work-made-for-hire arrangement rather than a collaboration arrangement.

Termination Provisions: As we say in the business, it's not a matter of whether collaborators or band members will break up but when. So you should agree up front what will happen when the collaboration ends. For example, what happens to the manuscript, the income, the expenses? What happens if the book needs to be revised?

Contract Checklist

❏ describe the work

❏ describe each person's contribution, the schedule of anticipated due dates, the form in which the contribution should be submitted, and the arrangements regarding how the contributors will share all financial and other responsibilities to develop the work

❏ state how long the collaboration agreement will remain in effect and, if the term expires or the contract is terminated, which, if any, clauses will remain in effect

❏ outline what happens if one of the contributors should become physically or mentally incapacitated or die during the term of the agreement

❏ set forth how artistic decisions will be made, namely, whether each contributor shares artistic control over the entire project, whether each person has individual control over his or her contribution, or whether one person has the final say about all such decisions

❏ state how business decisions will be made, namely, whether all contributors have a say, whether there will be a majority vote, or whether one contributor controls all business decisions

❏ describe what will happen if or when offered an agency or publishing agreement (if the contributors do not already have an agent or the publishing agreement isn't already entered into) and whether and under what circumstances self-publication is an option

❏ discuss how and when intellectual property rights will be applied for or registered

❏ address how derivative works will be managed

❏ enumerate what financial investment each party will make, whether expenses and investments will be recoupable and how revenues will be divided, and whether contributors receive income individually or whether one person collects on behalf of everyone and then distributes payments

❏ set forth how contributors will be credited in the work and in advertisements and publicity related to the work

❑ address the circumstances under which the agreement can be terminated

❑ declare what law shall apply in the case of a dispute and whether the parties must submit to arbitration

❑ include any other provisions that further define the rights and responsibilities of the contributors

9 The Work-Made-for-Hire Agreement

As explained in chapter 4, a copyright generally exists in a work as soon as it is created in a fixed and tangible form. The creator of the work owns and controls the bundle of rights associated with copyright. An exception to that rule is the work-made-for-hire doctrine, in which the creator is not the owner for purposes of copyright protection. The Copyright Act provides strict guidelines that determine whether a work-made-for-hire situation exists.

Work made for hire can occur in two contexts: that involving employers and employees and that involving independent contractors. In the first, work made for hire is done by employees within the scope of their employment. In the second, an independent contractor is specially commissioned to perform work for one of the following purposes only:

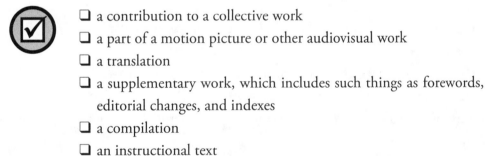

- ❏ a contribution to a collective work
- ❏ a part of a motion picture or other audiovisual work
- ❏ a translation
- ❏ a supplementary work, which includes such things as forewords, editorial changes, and indexes
- ❏ a compilation
- ❏ an instructional text
- ❏ a test
- ❏ answer material for a test
- ❏ a sound recording
- ❏ an atlas

Furthermore, the work performed by the independent contractor is considered to be work made for hire only if the contractor and the hiring person both agree to such—*before* the work begins.

Because the existence of work made for hire depends on the relationship of the parties involved, the first question to answer is whether the creator is an employee or an independent contractor.

Employee: In the employer-employee relationship, the employer controls the work product, work site, work schedule, and assignments; provides the equipment used to perform the work; pays the employee a regular salary and takes appropriate deductions; and so forth. For example, a staff writer is an employee of a newspaper company. In that situation, the newspaper company and not the staff writer owns the copyright of all work produced by the writer during his or her employment.

Independent contractor: Unlike employees, independent contractors maintain control over how the work they do is done. Independent contractors are in business for themselves. They provide their own equipment, and set their own hours and work schedules. They may refer to themselves as business owners, freelancers, self-employed, or consultants. They are their own bosses.

If you want an independent contractor to contribute to your product, and you want to retain copyright to his or her contribution, then, as stated earlier, you must agree to a work-made-for-hire arrangement before the work begins. You will find a sample agreement in Appendix B, but here's a checklist of important items that should be included in any work-made-for-hire agreement:

- ❑ the name, type of entity (corp., LLC, etc.), and address of each party
- ❑ a paragraph that sets forth the complete description of the work and the amount of compensation involved
- ❑ a list of all rights included, which should be the entire bundle of rights
- ❑ a statement that the creator has no rights in the work created or in the work in which the creation is used
- ❑ an assignment provision that assigns all rights, in case the work-made-for-hire agreement fails for any reason
- ❑ representations (specific facts about the work product—that it is original, for example) and warranties (an obligation by the person making representations that the facts either as stated or as implied are in fact correct)
- ❑ a confidentiality provision

❑ a clause that addresses what happens if the work is not completed or if you stop work before the independent contractor completes it

❑ due dates

❑ a clause dealing with information you give to the independent contractor in order to create the work and all work product, which should remain your property

❑ signature lines for all parties

10 The Agency Agreement

 An agency agreement is (usually) a straightforward and succinct document that details the rules which will govern your relationship with the agency as long as the agreement is in force. It is particularly important to understand that the terms you agree to today will be the ones you will be required to follow for a long, long time. So, even if the contract is only a few pages long, you must take the time to go over every word. Ask questions of all the professionals involved in the transaction. And contact a lawyer to review the terms with you and negotiate the most favorable terms for you so that you can live with them comfortably over the long term.

The basic terms provide that you designate the agent or agency as your exclusive agent to represent your rights (either all rights or only those limited rights set forth in the agreement), for a specific time referred to as the term of the agreement, in a specific area referred to as the territory; that all money owed to you from the sale of your rights will be sent first to your agent; and that he or she (or the agency) is entitled to a percentage, known as the commission, of that compensation—usually 10 to 20 percent of your gross receipts (with the average being 15 percent)—before he or she distributes the remainder to you.

Although there is some disagreement (usually from newly formed or small agencies) about whether writers should pay any fees to agents, it is generally considered unethical for a writer to have to pay any reading fees (monthly, annually, or otherwise). But reimbursement or advance payment of extraordinary expenses may be appropriate (for travel, hand-delivery charges, or anything above and beyond ordinary business expenses). The agency business is a risk-reward business; the agent is supposed to make an up-front investment in your work in order to earn 10 to 20 percent of your hard-earned money for as long as the book exists, which she will earn if her efforts are successful and she sells your book. So writers beware; make sure any fees are closely scrutinized and warranted.

Clauses to Consider

Rights: As with the other agreements, pay close attention to this paragraph in your agency agreement. An agency's standard agreement will likely include a comprehensive rights clause that includes all books in all genres throughout the world in all languages. If that is not your intention, or as can be the case with smaller agencies, if the agent does not have an extensive track record in exploiting such a vast array of rights, then consider negotiating a more limited clause covering a smaller territory, a shorter term, or limits in terms of language (English) or a particular genre.

Representations and Warranties: In this paragraph the parties make certain representations of what they will do or provide, and make certain warranties that the facts as stated or reasonably inferred are accurate. This additional step may seem unnecessary to the layperson, but reps and warranties (as they are commonly called) are an insurance policy of sorts, to assure the other party that he or she can rely on the facts presented, facts such as the party has the right to enter into the agreement or is a company duly authorized and validly existing under the relevant state law.

Representations and Warranties. The Author warrants and represents that the Author has the right to enter into this Agreement and that the Author does not have, nor will the Author hereafter enter into any agreement or incur any obligation in conflict herewith. The Agent warrants and represents that it will market the Author's properties, use its best efforts to negotiate the best available terms and conditions on Author's behalf, and use its best efforts in the foregoing for the purpose of securing deals based on the exploitation of Author's properties.

Commission: The agent's commission—the amount the agent receives from revenues generated by your work—will be detailed in the agreement. The range is 10 percent to 20 percent but in most cases is 15 percent.

Coterminous/Coextensive Provisions: The agreement may have a provision that essentially changes the term of the agency agreement to run for the same time and in the same manner as the term of any contract entered into. So for example, even if your agency agreement is for three years, it may in fact run for the entire term of copyright if your publishing agreement runs that long (and it usually does). Eventually, the "out of print" provisions in a publishing agreement kick in if properly drafted, but you should pay particular attention to a coterminous/coextensive provision. And choose your agent wisely, because this relationship could last longer than most marriages!

Coterminous/Co-Extensive Provisions: The term hereof shall match the duration of and be automatically extended and re-extended with respect to any specific engagement, property, or material whenever and so long as any contract or contracts covered by this Agreement (as hereinafter defined) relating to such specific engagement, property, or material, shall be or continue in effect, including any and all exercises of options, extensions, renewals, modifications, substitutions for and additions to such contract(s), and for one (1) year thereafter.

Contract Checklist

At a minimum, the agency agreement should include:

❑ a clear and specific transfer-of-rights clause that details the rights given to the agent, the length of time the transfer lasts (term), the area that the agreement covers (territory, such as regional, national, international, world), and which rights you are reserving for yourself (or an "all rights not specifically mentioned are hereby reserved . . ." clause)

❑ amount of the agent's commission, whether it is based on gross or net compensation, and the deadline by which the agent must pay you the amounts due to you

❑ what, if any, expenses you are responsible for

❑ author and agent representations and warranties, especially that the agency will use its "best efforts" to sell the author's work

❑ power-of-attorney clause granting the agent the right to collect money on your behalf and to endorse checks, and to deduct the agency commission from that money

❑ assignment provisions

❑ termination provisions

❑ accounting, author statements, and auditing provisions

❑ a provision that indicates what law applies to interpret and enforce the agreement

Watch for automatic renewal provisions and negotiate them carefully or strike them altogether. And be sure to exclude any pre-existing deals you have with publishers from the deals covered by the agency agreement.

11 The Publishing Agreement

 In simple terms, a publishing agreement (also referred to as a book deal or contract) is a legal arrangement between an author and publisher. The author agrees to transfer to the publisher certain rights in the bundle of rights associated with her copyrighted manuscript, and the publisher agrees, in turn, to pay for the costs to publish the manuscript. In exchange, both parties receive some financial gain (the publisher reaping the lion's share, of course). By agreeing to pay for all costs of publishing (in the best-case scenario), in effect the publisher becomes an investor in the author's manuscript. The publisher is entitled to recoup the initial investment and to take a sizeable percentage of the income generated by sales and licensing of the work. The author often receives an advance against royalties (explained below) and a percentage of royalties and subsidiary rights income.

Many complaints are hurled at publishers for the seemingly unfair percentages of income they earn and the extensive rights they retain in publishing deals. But the publishing industry, like any industry, is very much a bottom-line business. And it is often a challenge for publishers to make profits because the majority of publishing agreements do not earn out, meaning that most publishers (small and big alike) do not earn back their initial investment, which includes the author's advance. This advance is a recoupable payment to the author before publication; it is offset by income from sales after publication; in other words, it's a quasi loan from the publisher to the author.

Generally, publishers create a Profit and Loss Statement to anticipate the costs of publication (prepress, printing, marketing, and promotion) and projected earnings, taking into account the proposed market and demand for the book; sales numbers if the book being acquired is a previously self-published book, for example; industry discounts of at least 50 percent; and returns of at least 20 percent. Publishers select a figure based on the net profit number, a figure they reasonably believe they will recoup from sales, and, in most cases, pay the author an advance based on some percentage of that anticipated profit. A book earns out when all costs, including the advance, are recouped from sales and licensing revenue.

But it is not uncommon for a book to go out of print after selling only five thousand copies. Imagine the following scenario: You sign an agreement with a major publishing company in New York for hardcover rights to your fiction manuscript. You receive a modest $60,000 advance (and in some genres sums are not modest but insulting at $5,000 or less!) and a standard royalty schedule of 10 percent for the first five thousand copies sold. If the net retail price is $24.95, gross profit on 5,000 copies would be $124,750. Applying the average industry discount of 50 percent reduces net profits to $62,375. Now apply the loss of income for returns of 20 percent, which reduces the net profits to $49,900. Subtract $20,000 in production costs (not including your advance), and $29,900 remains. Your royalty of 10 percent yields $2,990, against which your author advance is applied, and the publisher is still in the hole to recoup the remaining $57,010 paid in advance to you.

But do not cry for the publisher just yet because it does pocket $26,910. In addition, the example does not account for the licensing of subsidiary rights like book club rights, mass market rights, audio book rights, electronic rights, and so forth. The point is that the publishing industry is a dollars-and-cents business from the publisher's perspective. And despite your core values as a creative spirit who values words over profits, if you intend to be successful in this business, you must begin to understand and embrace the bottom line too.

Key Clauses

There are as many variations in the precise terms of a publishing agreement as there are publishing agreements. But certain key terms should exist in every contract. This section focuses on key clauses in a standard publishing agreement. You will find a complete sample form in Appendix B and in the Forms Library on the CD-ROM.

Understanding the nature, purpose, meaning, and effect of the key clauses in the contract is an important first step in breaking down complex legal terminology into common understanding. Of course, literary law is a vast and complex subject. Accordingly, this section is merely a broad overview of some of the most common and essential clauses in a publishing agreement. Compare the discussion that follows to the corresponding clause in the sample contract.

Introductory Paragraph: Most contracts begin with an introductory paragraph that sets forth the names and legal capacities of the parties as well as the effective date of the agreement. It may also include their addresses.

This Agreement is made this ___ day of _____, 2007 (The "Agreement"), by and between _____, an individual (hereinafter referred to as AUTHOR) located at _ _____, and ABC Publishing Company, a corporation (hereinafter referred to as PUBLISHER) whose principal place of business is located at _____, concerning a work presently entitled _____ (as described in greater detail below).

Grant of Rights: The grant of rights clause is where the author assigns copyright to the publisher.

 ### Grant of Rights

The Author hereby grants, transfers, and assigns to the Publisher for the full term of copyright the exclusive right to publish in hardback and paperback editions (the Primary Rights) and sell throughout the world in the English language the literary work presently entitled _____ (hereinafter called Work). The Author also grants and assigns to the Publisher the exclusive subsidiary rights to said Work, with exclusive authority to license said rights in all countries and in all languages.

Thus, this clause defines the rights the author will assign to the publisher, the nature of the rights, the applicable territory, and the amount of time the contract will remain in effect. The assignment of rights means that the publisher and not the author is the owner of whatever rights are conveyed during the term of the agreement. Generally, the grant of rights is exclusive to one publisher. Sometimes authors assign the entire bundle of rights by way of a broad, all-inclusive grant of rights such as the one noted in the sample clause, but you need not transfer all of your rights to the publisher. And you should always include a reservation-of-rights clause after the grant of rights as follows:

 All rights not expressly granted to the Publisher are hereby reserved by the Author.

Keep in mind that if you have or intend to have a Web site in the future, you should consider reserving rights in your domain name, and protecting your ability to sell author copies (watch for a clause that restricts this ability) and to provide information from your Web site with no limitation by or compensation to the publisher.

In addition, you should grant to a publisher only the rights you believe the publisher is capable of exploiting to your benefit. A publisher may, as a matter of course, seek to control all rights. But why grant motion picture or dramatic rights, for instance, if the publisher has neither successfully exploited those rights in the past nor has established relationships in those fields to exploit the rights successfully in the future. Although licensing motion picture or dramatic rights is speculative in most cases, it may be best to retain them and sell them to others who are in a better position to successfully exploit them. The point is, do not just go along simply for the sake of appearing agreeable. And even if you cannot negotiate to keep certain sub-rights, you can use them as a bargaining chip to negotiate other clauses to your advantage.

Some authors negotiate a more limited grant of rights for a particular work (for example, the hardcover rights, paperback rights, mass market rights, book club rights, foreign rights, large print rights, and a host of others). Doing so allows the author to shop the remaining rights and negotiate a deal (based on the strength of the first edition) with the same publisher or with a different one. The grant of rights can also be limited by language (for example, the English-speaking market) or by territory (North America only, for example).

Description of the Work: The Description of the Work clause is deceptively simple, and you should pay close attention to its provisions. In many cases the description is basic and general, providing an approximate page length or a specified number of words, the general genre, the topic, and the tentative title. But you should consider including more information or incorporating the book proposal and perhaps sample chapters as an attachment (known as an Exhibit) to the agreement. This revision is important to consider if the publisher has the right to reject the manuscript and terminate the agreement if it is not "acceptable to the publisher in form and content" (see *Delivery* and *Acceptance* sections below). If the publisher has this basically subjective right to reject, you need to be reasonably certain that your understanding of what the manuscript will contain is consistent with the publisher's expectation of what you will submit. Problems can result when the publisher's expectations for the manuscript differ from the author's understanding. Therefore, sometimes a more detailed description benefits both parties.

Delivery and Acceptance of the Manuscript

Author shall deliver to Publisher on or before _____, 2007 (the "Delivery Date"), one (1) original hardcopy of the complete Work and one (1) copy on computer disk, together with any supplementary materials (including, without limitation, drawings, illustrations, photographs, maps, graphs, tables). If Author fails to deliver the Work by the delivery date, after a grace period of thirty (30) days (or such other period as shall be determined by the Publisher and agreed to in writing by both parties), Publisher may demand the return of all sums paid to or on behalf of Author by Publisher in connection with the Work, and this Agreement shall terminate. Upon termination under these circumstances, Author may not resubmit the Work (or any part thereof) or a similar work to any other publisher without first offering it to Publisher under the same terms and conditions contained in this Agreement.

Publisher shall inform the Author in writing as to whether the complete Work is acceptable to Publisher in form and content within ninety (90) days of receipt of the complete Work. If Publisher determines the Work is unacceptable but capable of cure, Publisher and Author shall agree upon a time for revision ("Revision Period") and Publisher shall provide to Author written comments explaining the necessary revisions. If Publisher determines that the first submission cannot be cured or that the revision created during the Revision Period is still unacceptable, Publisher shall have the right, in Publisher's sole discretion, to reject the Work by giving written notice to the Author.

If the Work is rejected, Author shall keep fifty percent (50%) of the advances paid to date and shall return the remaining fifty percent (50%) within one year of rejection. The Author may submit the Work to a third party, provided that Author shall remain obligated to repay to Publisher the amounts retained by Author from all proceeds from any sale of license by the Author of rights of any nature in the Work to a third party (the "First Proceeds").

The clauses dealing with delivery and acceptance of the manuscript are important and sometimes problematic parts of the contract.

Delivery: The contract should specifically state the date that the manuscript is due and in what form or forms (hardcopy, e-mail attachment, disk) it should be delivered, as well as any technical specifications (margin width, one-sided, double-spaced) required by the publisher. In addition, any supplementary materials expected to accompany the manuscript (photographs, illustrations, and other materials created by someone else that may require permission from a third party to use) should be noted in this section.

Supplementary Materials and Indexing

Be sure to check the fine print in the contract about supplementary materials (photographs, illustrations, artwork, interview excerpts, and so forth). If your work includes supplementary materials, a publisher will require that you get permission from the owner to use them. Also, if you transferred to an agent rights that you intend to give to the publisher, you will need permission from the agent to do so (often covered by an agency clause inserted into the contract). Lastly, if your work needs an index, the publisher will require either that you provide it when you deliver your complete manuscript (or some time thereafter as agreed to) or that you pay for the expense of having the index written.

First, confirm whether you are responsible for (1) obtaining and (2) paying for supplementary materials. Generally, publishers require in the contract that authors seek and pay for the cost of obtaining permissions, although sometimes the publisher will agree to actually obtain permission since it may be in a better position to do so. Publishers will also ask you to pay for illustrations, artwork, maps, indexing, and so forth. But these requirements can (and should) be negotiated so that either the publisher pays or the costs are split between publisher and author. If you cannot change the terms, try to get the publisher to advance you the money and to recoup its expenses from your royalty account so that you do not have to pay any out-of-pocket expenses.

For a sample permissions form, see Appendix B.

Acceptance: At times, a publisher or an editor at a large publishing company will offer a book deal in response to a query letter, proposal, or pitch. Based on that material, the editor will formulate certain expectations of the final manuscript. If those expectations are not adequately spelled out in writing and conveyed to the author, the finished product will not be what the editor expected.

Another possibility is that although the editor conveys his or her expectations clearly, the author, who was great at crafting a pitch, is ill equipped to finish the manuscript. To deal with these contingencies, publishers often demand that the manuscript be delivered in a form and content satisfactory to the publisher. Clearly, this is subjective and gives a publisher wide latitude to reject a manuscript. Some authors negotiate for a more objective clause that sets forth criteria which, if met, will render the manuscript fit for publication. An alternate approach is to give the author the opportunity to cure the defect (revise the manuscript) based on the publisher's comments.

Secondary (or Subsidiary) Rights: Ordinarily, the primary right granted to a book publisher is the right to publish the manuscript in book form. This right can include all print rights or, for instance, only hardback, trade paper, or mass market rights. Some publishers, however, seek electronic, spoken-word edition, Internet, audio, and book club rights in the primary grant. Traditionally, these rights were considered subsidiary or secondary to the primary right to publish the manuscript in book form. But as new media are developed and used to publish works in other forms, publishers will more aggressively try to control all known and future uses. Case law, however, suggests that unless the rights are expressly stated, they will not be transferred, which runs contrary to the "future media" clause in most publishing agreements.

You (or your agent, if you've transferred the rights to the agent) may also assign secondary or subsidiary rights to the publisher so that the publisher can exploit the Work in ways that may be less important (but still valuable) to the publisher, such as mass market paperback rights, book club rights, and foreign and translation rights, and in media *other than* books, such as motion picture and television rights, stage plays (dramatic rights), electronic rights, performance rights, and more. Again, keep in mind that any of these rights could be included in the primary rights clause if the publisher primarily intends to exploit them. Therefore the list of subsidiary rights below is not etched in stone but serves as a guide for your information.

Subsidiary rights include:

- ❑ Periodical rights (first or second serial)
- ❑ Book club rights
- ❑ Dramatic rights (theatrical rights)

- ❏ Motion picture and TV rights
- ❏ Videocassett.e and audiocassette rights
- ❏ Radio rights
- ❏ Merchandising (commercial tie-in) rights
- ❏ New technology
- ❏ Foreign translation rights
- ❏ Electronic rights
- ❏ Internet rights
- ❏ Mass market paperback rights

Subsidiary Rights Revenue: A sub-rights compensation clause could look like this:

The net revenues received from the exploitation of the enumerated subsidiary rights shall be shared fifty percent (50%) to the Author and fifty percent (50%) to the Publisher, except that the division of the net revenues from dramatic, motion picture, and television licenses shall be seventy-five percent (75%) to the Author and twenty-five percent (25%) to the Publisher.

One of the most important sections of a publishing contract deals with how you get paid. A publishing company can compensate an author in several different ways; sometimes the publisher uses one particular method of payment; at other times two or more methods are combined.

Advance: A more apt title for this clause would be "quasi-loan" because, as the word suggests and as stated above, this payment is an advance against future royalties. The advance is commonly paid in three installments, one-third on signing, one-third on delivery, and one-third on acceptance (or publication), although there are several variations on this theme, including half on signing and half on publication.

Royalties: Royalties are payments made by the publisher to the author based on money received from sales. Think of a royalty as a percentage of every book sale. Royalties do not ordinarily include monies earned from licensing agreements for the exploitation of subsidiary rights, as defined above.

Royalties are generally based on the retail price of the book. Royalty calculations can include escalations that attach higher rates to greater numbers of books sold. Additionally, some publishers opt to have separate royalty calculations for different editions. Typical escalations based on the U.S. cover price may look like this:

Hardback Rate	Trade Paper Rate	Mass Market Paperback
10% on first 5,000	8% on first 10,000	6 to 8% on first 150,000 copies
12½% on next 5,000	10% on all additional copies	
15% on all additional copies		8 to 10% on all additional copies

As stated above, publishers traditionally base the royalty rate on the retail or cover price. This is the price printed on the book. But a significant number of publishers have moved away from tradition and instead base royalty rates on the net price, which is the price actually received by the publisher. This break in tradition has occurred because of the rise of mandatory discounts within the industry to booksellers (20 to 40 percent), distributors (50 to 55 percent), and wholesalers and book clubs (as much as 80 percent).

When negotiating your royalty rate, try to secure a bonus structure for receiving what we call professional recognition. Professional recognition can be placement on a prominent best-seller list (*New York Times* or *Essence*); a literary prize that ultimately increases sales (Pulitzer); or any other honor, award, or achievement, such as signing a motion picture or TV deal.

Net Revenues: Sometimes publishers offer a percentage of net revenues instead of a sales royalty and licensing percentage scheme. This is most likely to be offered by independent publishers, who try to avoid the administrative hassles that accompany complex royalty calculations. Instead, the publisher will recoup its expenses and then split the remaining revenue based on a negotiated percentage.

Flat Rate: Although this is not a common option, some publishers offer a flat fee to purchase your manuscript. This may occur, for instance, in writing competitions where the prize is a lump sum plus publication, or for contributions to an anthology that are being paid for with money and not just with copies of the finished book.

Best-seller and Performance Bonuses: We always hear about the impressive six and seven figure advances coming from the big New York publishing companies. But, in my experience, that is the exception rather than the rule. When a star-turned-author or rising star with an existing sales base gets such a deal, that leaves little money for other writers seeking a deal. In fact, it is becoming all too common for publishing companies to offer paltry sums for two-book paperback fiction deals. Unfortunately, writers are taking the bait and watering down offers and expectations.

One way for writers and writer's representatives to overcome this trend and its negative impact on the bottom line is to forgo larger advances (front-end money) in negotiations, and negotiate best-seller and performance bonuses (back-end money). I have seen these provisions save deals and turn into win-win situations when the writer does prove herself with demonstrable sales or best-seller status.

Options: The options clause gives the publisher the first right to purchase (or refuse) the next work created by the author. A typical options clause might look like this:

> **Publisher shall have the right to acquire Author's next book-length work on terms to be mutually agreed upon by the parties. Author shall submit a detailed outline and sample chapter of the next book-length work to Publisher before submitting the work to any other publisher, and Publisher shall have a period of thirty days after receipt of said detailed outline and sample chapter (the Option Period) in which to review the submission and determine whether to exercise the option. The Option Period shall not begin to run earlier than sixty days after publication of the Work. If Publisher declines or fails to exercise its option by the expiration of the Option Period, then Author may submit the work to other publishers or otherwise dispose of the work, at Author's sole discretion.**

Note that in the example, the publisher has the right to purchase the next work on terms "to be mutually agreed upon by the parties." But most option clauses will state that the publisher can acquire the next work on the same terms as the existing agreement. If that is the case, the same option clause (and advance and royalty rates) will appear in the second contract and the third and so on, until the publisher decides not to exercise its option. So the two-book deal winds up being a multiple-book deal for the publisher, without an opportunity for the author to negotiate a more favorable deal based on success of the first or second book.

Of course the publisher wants as many opportunities as possible not only to recoup its sizable investment but also to benefit financially from the success of the work. On the other hand, you want to be in a position to negotiate a more lucrative and favorable deal if the initial work is successful. Therefore, this is an extremely important clause that should be negotiated carefully and comprehensively.

Revisions: The revisions clause is not appropriate for fiction, but appears for most non-fiction books. At first glance, many authors are put off by the revisions clause. But in reality, revising nonfiction keeps the information fresh and can extend the shelf life of the book. But you must take care to limit the revisions clause and to insert some protective provisions that seem to be conspicuously absent from the drafts of most publishing agreements (to the great detriment of the author). Those provisions appear in italics in the contract clause below.

The Author shall revise the Work (a Revised Work) *two (2) times* after initial publication and within one (1) year from the receipt of written request from the Publisher to do so. A Revised Work shall not substantially alter the original Work and further, *shall not constitute a new work for copyright and royalty escalation purposes.* In the event that the Author is unable or unwilling to provide a revision within one (1) year after the Publisher has requested it, or should the Author be deceased, the Publisher may have the revision made *at the Publisher's expense* (such expense to be recoupable from royalties) and may display, in the revised Work and in advertising, the name of the person or persons who perform the revision.

This clause, as drafted, builds in certain protections for authors. First, it limits the number of revisions. Second, it states that a revision will not be considered a new work for purposes of copyright term and royalty escalations. Authors do not want the term or number of books sold to begin from zero again. Third, authors should try to negotiate to have the publisher pay for the costs of revisions if the author does not or cannot revise the work when requested to do so.

Out-of-Print/Reversion Clause: The out-of-print clause is extremely important for several reasons. First, the definition of the term "out-of-print" determines when the rights revert back to the author, that is, when all rights in copyright of the published work are transferred back to the author from the publisher. Second, because of electronic publishing, including e-books, print-on-demand technology, online services, and interactive media, it can now be argued that the work will never go out of print because the electronic files and print-on-demand technology are not capable of being exhausted. Unfortunately, many publishing agreements are used over and over again without being updated to reflect current conditions. Therefore, a new definition of "out-of-print" must be included in publishing agreements today to account for new technologies and to protect authors.

The Work shall be considered to be out of print if it is not available in the United States through regular retail channels in the English language book form edition and not listed in the publisher's catalog; further availability through print-on-demand or other electronic or mechanical means alone does not make a book in print. In the event that the Publisher fails to keep the Work in print and the Author makes a written request of the Publisher to keep the Work in print, the Publisher shall, within sixty (60) days after receipt of that written request, notify the Author in writing of the Publisher's decision in the matter. If the Publisher elects to keep the Work in print, it shall have six (6) months thereafter to reprint and release the Work into ordinary sales channels. In the event that the Publisher elects not to keep the Work in print or fails to comply with the deadline of six (6) months (unless the failure is due to circumstances beyond its control), then this Agreement shall terminate and all rights granted to the Publisher shall revert immediately to the Author.

Special clause to address electronic versions of the Work

If Publisher sells no more than _____ copies of Author's Work in either electronic or downloadable format, or by means of print-on-demand technology, over any _____ consecutive-month period of this Agreement, then either party may terminate this Agreement upon thirty (30) days' notice in writing sent to the other party. Upon such termination, all rights granted under this Agreement, except the rights to dispose of existing copies, if any, including but not limited to electronic, printed, or audio copies, shall revert to Author, subject to all rights that may have been granted by Publisher to third parties under this Agreement, and Publisher shall have no further obligations or liabilities to Author except that Author's earned royalties shall be paid when and as due.

A Publisher's Duty to Publish: A publisher's duty to publish must be specifically addressed in the agreement. This includes what damages the author will receive if the publisher fails to publish as promised. In *Alternative Thinking Systems Inc. v. Simon & Schuster,* the court suggested that authors should receive, at a minimum, all advances paid to date and immediate reversion of rights. What would happen if the author has not received an advance remains an unanswered question.

Agent Clause: If you have an agent who has gotten you a publishing deal, there will be a paragraph in the publishing agreement appointing the agent as your representative to collect monies and to receive notices on your behalf. While this may seem like a standard innocuous clause, I caution writers to be on the lookout for what The Authors Guild has called the "interminable agency" clause.

In "Avoid Granting an Interminable Right to Represent Your Work," an article e-mailed to members on May 11, 2004, the Authors Guild warned authors to avoid the interminable agency clause. This clause, which often appears in the agency paragraph in a publishing agreement (but not in the author-agent agreement, in most cases), gives agents the exclusive right to receive royalties from works covered by the agreement for the entire term of copyright. At present, the term of copyright lasts for the life of the author plus seventy years.

The Author's Guild lists a number of valid reasons why this clause does not benefit either party. One of the most obvious and important reasons, from an author's perspective, is that an agent's rights should run coextensively and coterminously with the publishing agreement and should terminate when a work goes out of print, when presumably the benefit of the agent's work also ends. Of course most authors do not begrudge an agent's right to a commission when it is earned through the agent's substantial efforts to place a work with a publishing house. But giving any further compensation to the agent without a new rights sale, license, or other exploitation of the author's work is at best unfair and, in my opinion, borders on unconscionable.

As agents see it, they work on commission, and some literary properties sell quickly while others take a considerable amount of time and effort to shop. So agents will try to protect their interests by increasing their opportunity to recoup their investments and make a living. Nonetheless, there are so many ways an author can successfully challenge such a clause that the agent could easily spend more time embroiled in conflicts (and even litigation) with clients then he or she does making deals and finding new clients. Also, tracking and enforcing interminable rights for each client over many years seems to be an administrative burden and, quite frankly, an impossibility when it is unlikely the agency will even be in existence for the entire term of copyright (again, the author's life plus seventy years). Thus, the cons seem to far outweigh the pros when you think about the small amount of compensation (if any) that may be earned and paid to an agent after a work goes out of print.

So I recommend that authors and agents make sure that the agency paragraph in publishing agreements no longer includes the interminable agency clause, also known as a right coupled with an interest.

Accounting: Generally, publishing companies account, that is, send statements of copies sold and returns and revenues received, biannually, with any payments due made about one month later. But in the last few years my phone has been ringing off the hook with disgruntled authors and wayward publishers in arrears. Admittedly, this happens most often with small and independent presses who are not as fully capitalized as larger, more established houses. So if you are signing with a small company, consider including the following clause in the contract to protect yourself in case the payments are consistently late or missing altogether.

If any payments due to Author are in arrears for more than two accounting periods, Author shall have the right to demand immediate payment within thirty (30) days of all outstanding sums due. If payment is not made within such thirty day time period, all rights granted hereunder shall revert automatically back to Author and all legal and equitable remedies shall be preserved.

Contract Checklist

Publishing Agreement Checklist: A comprehensive publishing agreement will include all of the following clauses:

- ❑ Recitation
- ❑ Grant of Rights, including:
    - • Description of the Work and Rights Granted
    - • Territory
    - • Language
    - • Term
- ❑ Reservation of Rights
- ❑ Delivery and Acceptance of Work
- ❑ Additional Materials
- ❑ Permissions
- ❑ Representations and Warranties
- ❑ Duty to Publish
- ❑ Artistic Control
- ❑ Compensation Scheme (advance, royalties, net revenues, bonuses)
- ❑ Subsidiary Rights
- ❑ Payments
- ❑ Accounting
- ❑ Inspection of Books
- ❑ Copyright
- ❑ Indemnity
- ❑ Free Copies

❏ Revisions
❏ Reversion
❏ Remaindering
❏ Successors and Assigns
❏ Termination
❏ Agent Clause (if author has an agent)
❏ Promotion and Use of Author's Persona and Likeness
❏ Arbitration
❏ Notice
❏ Entire Agreement
❏ Waiver and Default
❏ Governing Law
❏ Signature Lines

12 Songwriting and Publishing Agreements

 Songwriting and publishing agreements involve the transfer of rights in a musical composition (the actual music and lyrics) to a music publisher to exploit the song on a greater scale than the writer could do in her own right. The two types of songwriter deals are single and exclusive. "Single" is actually a misnomer because a single song deal can actually involve more than one song. Songwriting deals do not involve rights in any actual performance, only in the underlying musical composition.

The songwriter assigns to the publisher full copyright ownership in the writer's musical compositions in exchange for publisher's administrative services to exploit the song or songs and collect and distribute revenues, including paying the writer's share of any nonperformance income.

 Performance versus Nonperformance Music Publishing Income

Performance income results from licensing revenues for the nondramatic live or broadcast public performance of a musical composition (at concerts, in bars, in elevators, or on the radio, for example) and is tracked, collected, and distributed by performance rights organizations: ASCAP, BMI, and SESAC. These organizations pay the writer and publisher separately and directly to members of their respective organizations. All other income resulting from exploiting a musical composition (for example, print, mechanical, electrical transcription, synchronization, and videogram licensing income) is collected by the music publisher and then distributed to the writer. Note that the music publisher will also be the songwriter if she self-publishes her own work.

In exchange, the publisher earns a publisher's share, which would otherwise also go to the songwriter in her capacity as a self-publisher. The publisher provides creative, promotional, and administrative services intended to enhance potential income opportunities (performance and nonperformance income) upon which the writer's and publisher's shares are based.

Savvy songwriters will negotiate to receive some part of the publisher's share of income. This is referred to as a "participation deal" (see the Co-Publishing Deal in Appendix B). In the case of participation deals, the songwriter receives not only the writer's entire share but receives a portion of the publisher's share as well. This is a very important opportunity that is negotiated depending on the strength of the writer's negotiating position.

When a writer participates in the publisher's share of royalties, the writer generally enters into both a songwriter's agreement to set forth the terms and conditions under which he receives his writer's share of revenues and a co-publishing agreement to set forth the terms and conditions under which the writer participates in the publisher's share of revenue. Sometimes, however, these agreements are merged into one document.

Single Song: Many provisions of the single song agreement mirror provisions in an exclusive agreement. But in the case of a single song agreement, the songwriter grants to the publisher full copyright ownership in one or a few specific musical compositions. The song or songs should be listed in an exhibit or schedule to the contract so it is clear which musical compositions are covered by the agreement.

Exclusive Song: Writer grants to the publisher full ownership in the copyright of any and all songs created during the term. An exclusive contract can also include a songwriter's existing songs, but these should be listed in an exhibit or schedule to the contract. Song publishers tend to offer these deals to songwriters who have demonstrated a successful track record of creating hit songs consistently or to songwriters who are also recording artists and have a viable opportunity under a recording contract to record and otherwise publish the songs they have written. In this case, entering into an exclusive arrangement reduces a publisher's overall transaction costs compared to having single song deals for each new song.

Exclusive deals usually include advances; some form of guaranteed income (weekly or monthly salary, for example); and access to publisher's recording facilities and connections, including access to other successful songwriters.

13 The Licensing Agreement

A licensing agreement sets forth terms that permit others the limited right to use your work. In contrast to an assignment (such as that in a publishing contract) where you, as the copyright owner, actually transfer the copyright to a new owner (the publisher), in a license you retain the copyright but give permission to the licensee to use the work in a certain way, for a certain time, and in a specified area.

Clauses to Consider

Description of Property: One of the most important clauses is the one that describes the property being licensed. As noted in the license checklist below, it is imperative to describe the property with specificity.

Grant of License: As with the description of property, the grant of license must be clear and specific. Here is a sample. See the form in Appendix B for more information.

Upon receipt of full payment pursuant to Paragraphs __ and __ below, Licensor grants to the Licensee the following [nonexclusive] [exclusive] rights in the Property for use as_____ in the _____ language for the [product] [publication] [purpose] tentatively titled _____. [For magazine, newspaper or similar contribution: For one-time North American serial rights].

Territory: The territory can be as narrowly defined as a region or as broadly defined as worldwide. The broader the territory, the more revenue the licensor should receive. Carefully negotiate this provision.

Reservation of Rights: The licensor should include a statement that reserves any rights not specifically granted in the license. This clause provides greater clarity and minimizes confusion as to what rights are being licensed.

Reservation of Rights. All rights not expressly granted hereunder are reserved to the Licensor, including but not limited to all rights in preliminary and supplementary materials [and all electronic rights. For purposes of this agreement, electronic rights are defined as rights in the digitized form of works that can be encoded, stored, and retrieved from such media as computer disks, CD-ROM, computer databases, and network servers].

Other Uses of Property: The licensor should require an additional license for any other uses of the licensed property not specifically permitted by the license.

If Licensee wishes to make any additional uses of the Property, Licensee shall request permission from the Licensor and make any such payments as are agreed to between the parties at that time.

Alteration of Property: Additionally, the licensor should forbid alternations of the property without his or her prior approval. Below is a typical alteration clause.

Licensee shall not make or permit any alterations, whether by adding or removing material from the Property, without the permission of the Licensor. Alterations shall be deemed to include the addition of any illustrations, photographs, sound, text, or computerized effects.

Contract Checklist
At a minimum the license should:

❏ describe with great specificity the property to be licensed
❏ note the date the property will be delivered to the licensee and in what form it must be delivered
❏ describe with great specificity the rights granted to the licensee, namely, setting forth exactly how the licensee is allowed to use the property and whether those rights are exclusive or nonexclusive
❏ note the language and geographical locations in which the property can be used and how long the license will remain in effect
❏ include a reservation-of-rights clause stating that any use not expressly granted in the license is reserved by you
❏ set forth the payment terms, which may include a lump sum license fee, advance, royalty schedule, license fees paid in installments, and so forth

❑ include provisions for copyright notice and credit

❑ address whether the licensee has the right to alter the property in any way

❑ include a confidentiality clause for any proprietary information disclosed to the licensee regarding the property or your business pursuits

❑ outline the ways each party can terminate the agreement

❑ discuss whether parties must submit to arbitration in case of a dispute

❑ discuss whether the license can be assigned by any party

❑ include the governing law

❑ include a no-agency clause

You should make sure that the license is comprehensive enough to secure rights in all intended uses. The *New York Times, Newsday,* and *Time* magazine (print publishers) and NEXIS and University Microfilms International (electronic publishers) learned this lesson the hard way. For a complete discussion on the leading cases on this issue, see my book *Literary Law Guide for Authors.*

14 Permissions and Releases

 Although the publishing agreement usually receives a lot of attention, you should be aware, as a Literary Entrepreneur, that other contracts relating to the publishing industry may also be significant for you. In fact, before entering into a publishing agreement with you, a publisher may ask you for copies of a licensing agreement or permissions form (if you have incorporated the work of others—pictures, illustrations, photographs, and so forth—in your book). In addition, if you are a nonfiction writer or need a release from a third party for some other reason, publishing companies require that you as the writer secure permissions and releases at your own expense prior to publication.

Permission Request

A permission request is basically a short-form license agreement that lists the property to be used, the purpose for the use, and so forth. It notes the publication information and credit information. Keep in mind that many large companies have a preferred method of requesting permission to use a copyrighted work. So you should contact the publisher or owner, if possible, before submitting a permission request. Also, keep in mind that others are not nearly as interested in your deadlines as you are. So begin the process of clearing permissions as soon as possible. It generally takes most publishing companies four to eight weeks to reply to a permission request.

Release Form

Nonfiction writers write about real life and real experiences. Whether they are writing memoir, biography, or news reports, nonfiction writers tell a story—a real story. So there are certain legal issues that nonfiction writers in particular should be aware of—in addition to the other issues raised in this book—before, during, and after the writing process.

What differentiates fiction from nonfiction is that fiction is not real; it is made up; it comes from the writer's imagination. Nonfiction, on the other hand, is factual or at least represents the author's opinions based on facts. Nonfiction consists of many genres, such as history, philosophy, biography, and memoir. And in many forms of nonfiction writing, the writer interviews subjects or writes about real people and experiences. And photographers photograph subjects whose pictures may be used in a book. In these cases, writers should secure release forms from all relevant parties to avoid rights of privacy and publicity claims, as well as possible trademark infringement, defamation, or other similar causes of action.

Contract Checklist

- ❑ At a minimum, the release should include:
- ❑ Complete description of the project in which the model or interviewee's image, likeness, or information will appear
- ❑ The form and manner of use
- ❑ The territory
- ❑ The term
- ❑ Method of revocation of consent, if applicable
- ❑ Statement that subject is not entitled to compensation
- ❑ Representation and warranty from subjects that they have the right and authority to sign the release

Appendix A Resources for Writers

Resource	Contact
Web Sites	
American Arbitration Association	www.adr.org
Copyright Clearance Center	www.copyright.**com**, not to be confused with copyright.**gov** (the official Copyright Office Web site listed below).
Copyright Office	www.copyright.gov
FindLaw.com: an online database of helpful legal resources on many different areas of the law	www.FindLaw.com
Legal Information Institute of Cornell University	www.law.cornell.edu
Library of Congress	www.loc.gov
United States Patent and Trademark Office	www.uspto.gov
Organizations	
Association of Authors and Publishers	www.authorsandpublishers.org
The Authors Guild	www.authorsguild.org
National Association of Women Writers	www.naww.org

National Writers Union	www.nwu.org
PMA, The Independent Book Publishers Association	www.pma-online.org
Small Publishers, Artists, and Writers, Network (SPAWN)	www.spawn.org
Small Publishers Association of North America (SPAN): an organization whose mission is "to advance the image and profits of independent publishers through education and marketing opportunities"	www.spannet.org
Women's National Book Association	www.wnba-books.org
Writers Guild of America	www.wga.org

Appendix B Forms

Collaboration Agreement
Contracts Companion for Writers, by Tonya M. Evans-Walls
www.LiteraryLawGuide.com

COLLABORATION AGREEMENT

THIS COLLABORATION AGREEMENT ("Agreement") is entered into as of the
_____ day of _____, 20 _____, (the "Effective Date") between
_____, a [enter capacity], located at _____
(hereinafter referred to as "Collaborator 1") and _____, a
[enter capacity], located at _____ (hereinafter referred to as
"Collaborator 2") regarding a project presently titled [insert working title of the
project] (the "Work").

TERMS

1. <u>Description of the Work</u>. The Work shall be approximately _____ words on
the subject of _____.
Materials other than text shall include _____.

[NOTE: Consider attaching a synopsis or outline of the Work and any other contributions to the Work.]

2. <u>Term</u>. The term for this Agreement shall be the duration of the copyright,
pursuant to the Copyright Act, in effect on the Effective Date, as extended by any
renewals or extensions thereof (the "Term").

3. <u>No Agency</u>. The parties to this Agreement are independent of one another,
and nothing contained in this Agreement shall make a partnership, agency, or joint
venture between them.

4. <u>Collaboration</u>. Each party agrees to cooperate with the other as joint authors
of the Work, to share equally in all tasks and responsibilities as may be necessary to
complete the Work, and to do what is necessary to secure its publication and other
exploitation, including research, writing and editing of the Work. To clarify the
respective duties of each party, the responsibilities shall be divided as follows:

 (a) Collaborator 1 shall be responsible for [include this collaborator's
responsibilities and what, if any, supplementary materials he/she will supply.]

 (b) Collaborator 2 shall be responsible for [include this collaborator's

Collaboration Agreement
Contracts Companion for Writers, by Tonya M. Evans-Walls
www.LiteraryLawGuide.com

responsibilities and what, if any, supplementary materials he/she will supply.]

(c)   This Agreement shall remain in effect for the duration of the Term (unless otherwise terminated before such time), and shall be binding upon each party's heirs and successors. In the event of the death or disability of either party that will prevent completion of his or her respective portion of the Work, or of a revision thereof or a sequel thereto, the other party shall have the right to complete that portion or to hire a third party to complete that portion and shall adjust the authorship credit to reflect the revised authorship arrangements. The deceased or disabled party shall receive payments pursuant to Paragraph 5 pro rata to the proportion of his or her work completed or, in the case of a revision or sequel, shall receive payments pursuant to Paragraph 5 after deduction for the cost of revising or creating the sequel with respect to his or her portion of the Work. In that case, the active party shall have the sole power to license and contract with respect to the Work, and approval of the personal representative, heirs, or conservator of the deceased or disabled party shall not be required. If all parties are deceased, the respective heirs or personal representatives shall take the place of the parties for all purposes.

(d)   Each party shall complete his or her contribution to the Work by _____, 20 ___, or by the date for delivery of the manuscript as specified in a publishing agreement entered into pursuant to Paragraph 12 below (the "Due Date"). In the event either party fails to complete his or her contribution to the Work by the Due Date, subject to subparagraph (c) above, a reasonable extension of time may be agreed to, or, in the alternative, the parties may agree to allow the non-defaulting party to complete the Work as if the defaulting party were deceased or disabled.

5.   <u>Division of Income and Expenses</u>. Income and expenses generated by or on behalf of the Work shall be divided as follows:

(a)   *Division of Income*. Net Income, defined as gross income as reduced by reasonable expenses, shall be divided equally between the parties [or insert other payment provisions] and paid directly to each party (or his or her designee). If either party receives income payable to the other party, the receiving party shall make immediate payment to the other party of such amounts as are due hereunder.

(b)   *Division of Expenses*. Expenses to produce the Work shall be divided equally between the parties [or insert other expense provisions]. Each party shall provide written proof of expenses and maintain a proper accounting of such expenses and corresponding payments. Unless otherwise provided, the parties' expenses shall be reimbursed from the first proceeds received, including but not limited to advances.

Collaboration Agreement
Contracts Companion for Writers, by Tonya M. Evans-Walls
www.LiteraryLawGuide.com

6.   Artistic Decisions.

(a)   Each party shall have artistic control over his or her portion of the Work. [Artistic control of the entire Work shall be exercised by _____.]

(b)   The parties shall share ideas and make their work-in-progress available to the other to facilitate completion of the Work. Except as otherwise provided in this Agreement, neither party shall at any time make any changes in the portion of the Work created by the other party without their consent.

7.   Business Decisions.

(a)   All editorial, business and other decisions affecting the Work, which require consent, shall be made jointly by the parties, and no agreement regarding the Work shall be valid without the signatures of both parties. The parties agree to reasonably consult with each other on such matters, and agree not to unreasonably withhold such consent to any decisions or agreements. In the event that the parties cannot mutually agree, the ultimate decision will be made by [_____].

(b)   Each party agrees that any communication by him or her to or from any editor, publisher or other industry professional, including an agent so long as both parties are represented by the same agent, must be promptly communicated to the other party.

8.   Copyright, Trademarks and Other Proprietary Rights.

(a)   The parties agree [that the work of each contributor shall be copyrighted in the names of each respective party and] that upon completion of each party's contribution, such contributions shall be merged into a joint work with a jointly owned copyright.

(b)   It is further agreed that trademarks, rights in characters, titles, and similar ongoing rights (collectively referred to as "Proprietary Rights") shall be owned jointly and equally by both parties.

9.   Derivative Works.

(a)   No derivative work based on the Work (as defined by the Copyright Act, as revised) shall be developed, created or exploited without the equal

Collaboration Agreement
Contracts Companion for Writers, by Tonya M. Evans-Walls
www.LiteraryLawGuide.com

participation of each party. However, if either party declines to participate in such a derivative work, then the other party shall be free to go forward on his or her own, and the non-participating collaborator shall be entitled to receive out of any Net Income of such derivative works, one-half (1/2) of the amount that would have been payable to the non-participating collaborator if the derivative work had been jointly prepared.

(b)   Material of any and all kinds developed or obtained in the course of creating the work shall be [jointly owned] [the property of the party who developed or obtained it].

10.   Agent. [The parties have each entered into an agency agreement with respect to the Work with the following agent:_____.]
The parties agree to seek an agency agreement [not to seek an agency agreement]. Any agency contract shall be mutually acceptable to and entered into in the names of and signed by each party, each of whom shall comply with and perform all required contractual obligations.

11.   Publisher; Licenses. [The parties have entered into a publishing agreement with respect to the Work with the following publisher:_____.]
The parties agree to seek a publishing agreement [not to seek an publishing agreement]. Any publishing agreement shall be mutually acceptable to and entered into in the names of and signed by each party, each of whom shall comply with and perform all required contractual obligations.

If a mutually agreeable publishing contract for initial publication of the Work is not entered into with a publisher by _____, 20_____, then both parties shall have the option to:

(a)   Jointly self-publish the Work and to enter into a separate publishing agreement to set forth the terms and conditions thereof.

(b)   Terminate this Agreement, pursuant to the procedures set forth in paragraph 13. Each party shall fully inform the other party of all negotiations for such a publishing agreement or with respect to the negotiation of any other licenses or contracts pursuant to this Agreement. The disposition of any right, including the grant of any license, shall require written agreement between both parties. Each party shall receive a copy of any contract, license, or other document relating to this Agreement.

12.   Authorship Credit. The credit line for the Work shall appear as follows wherever authorship credit is given in the Work or in promotion, advertising, or other

Collaboration Agreement
Contracts Companion for Writers, by Tonya M. Evans-Walls
www.LiteraryLawGuide.com

ancillary uses:_____.

13.   Termination. Except as provided in paragraph 4(c) above, the parties agree to follow the following procedures, if necessary, to terminate this Agreement:

(a)   If any party withdraws from the collaboration before the final manuscript of the Work is fully completed and accepted for publication for publisher, or, in the case of a self-published Work, before the Work has gone to print (the "Withdrawing Party"), then the rights of the Withdrawing Party (including but not limited to the rights to copyright and financial participation, if any) shall be determined by written agreement signed by all parties, or, if such an agreement cannot be reached, pursuant to the terms of paragraph 16 below.

(b)   If the parties determine that they are unable, for any reason, to complete the Work despite their best efforts to do so, then they will submit to arbitration as provided in Paragraph 16 below, to determine the rights and responsibilities of each party at that time to terminate the collaboration efforts fairly and amicably.

14.   Representations and Warranties; Indemnity. Each party warrants and represents to the other that his or her respective contribution(s) to the Work are original (or that appropriate permissions have been obtained) and do not libel or otherwise violate any right of any person or entity, including but not limited to rights of copyright, publicity, or privacy. Each party indemnifies and holds the other harmless from and against any and all claims, actions, liability, damages, costs, and expenses, including reasonable legal fees and expenses, incurred by the other as a result of the breach of such warranties, representations, and undertakings.

15.   Assignment. This Agreement shall not be assignable by either party hereto, provided, however, that after completion of the Work, either party may assign the right to receive income pursuant to Paragraph 5 by giving written notice to the other party.

16.   Arbitration. All disputes arising under this Agreement shall be submitted to confidential binding arbitration and shall be settled in accordance with the rules of the American Arbitration Association. Judgment upon the arbitration award may be entered in any court having jurisdiction thereof.

17.   Jurisdiction. This Agreement shall be governed by the laws of the State of

_____.

Collaboration Agreement
Contracts Companion for Writers, by Tonya M. Evans-Walls
www.LiteraryLawGuide.com

18.   Non-Disclosure and Non-Competition.

(a)   Each party agrees to hold in trust and confidence all material and information disclosed by one party to the other in connection with the Work, and not to disclose any such material or information to any third party without the prior written consent of the other. All such information and materials shall be regarded as proprietary trade secrets jointly owned and controlled by both parties.

(b)   Each party agrees not to prepare, or to participate in the preparation of, any other work that directly competes with or injures the sales of the Work during the Term without the signed written consent of the other party, such consent not to be unreasonably withheld.

19.   Infringement. In the event of an infringement of the Work, the parties shall have the right to sue jointly for the infringement and, after deducting the expenses of bringing suit, to share equally in any recovery [or insert other recovery provisions]. If either party chooses not to join in the suit, the other party may proceed and, after deducting all the expenses of bringing the suit, any recovery shall be shared between the parties as follows: _____.

20.   Entire Agreement. This Agreement shall be binding upon the parties hereto, their heirs, successors, assigns, and personal representatives. This Agreement constitutes the entire understanding between the parties. Only an instrument in writing signed by both parties can modify its terms. Further, a waiver of any breach of any of the provisions of this Agreement shall not be construed as a continuing waiver of other breaches of the same or other provisions hereof.

21.   Miscellaneous Provisions. Each party shall do all acts and sign all documents required to effectuate this Agreement.

IN WITNESS WHEREOF, the parties hereto have signed this Agreement as of the date first set forth above.

_____   _____
[Collaborator 1]   [Collaborator 2]

SSN: _____   SSN: _____

Work-Made-for-Hire Agreement
Contracts Companion for Writers, by Tonya M. Evans-Walls
www.LiteraryLawGuide.com

Work-Made-for-Hire Agreement

Patsi Pen
123 Champagne Lane
Philadelphia, PA 19199

DATE

Dear Ms. Pen,

Whereas you have agreed to prepare the Work (as hereinafter defined), this letter, when executed by the parties, will constitute an agreement ("Agreement") between Moe Doe ("I" or "me") and you ("you") with respect to the following:

1. I hereby commission you to prepare an original [literary/artistic] work [short description] (the "Work"), as further explained hereinbelow. You accept such commission and undertake to produce the Work in accordance with my instructions and under my editorial supervision and guidelines.

2.   (a) You agree that no later than the Final Due Date specified in subparagraph (c)(iii) below, you will deliver to me the complete Work and related materials (the "Materials") in final form in [describe specific manner and form for delivery].

    (b) The Work is described as follows: [description]

    (c) You agree to deliver the Work and the Materials on the following schedule:

        (i) A rough draft of the Work no later than _____.

        (ii) The complete and final Work and related Materials, if any, by _____ ("Final Due Date").

3.   (a) If you deliver the complete and final Work on or before the Final Due Date, I shall, within ten (10) days after such delivery, notify you whether the final Work as delivered is satisfactory and acceptable, and, if it is accepted by me, you will be paid pursuant to Paragraph 6 below.

    (b) If you fail to timely create and deliver the acceptable Work (including the Materials) on or before the due dates specified in Paragraph 2 above, I may engage another person or entity to assist in completing the Work or make other arrangements as I deem acceptable to keep the Work on schedule or to make it complete and satisfactory. In such event the cost of such arrangements may be charged against any sums due to you hereunder.

Work-Made-for-Hire Agreement
Contracts Companion for Writers, by Tonya M. Evans-Walls
www.LiteraryLawGuide.com

(c) If the Work and/or the Materials as delivered are not acceptable to me in my sole discretion, I will specify the deficiencies in a notice to you sent to via electronic mail or the address listed above. If I advise you of unacceptability, within ten (10) days after such notice you will submit either (i) revised, acceptable Work and Materials, or (ii) a proposed plan and delivery schedule for revising the Work and Materials. Acceptance of such revised Work and Materials or proposed plan and delivery schedule will be at my sole discretion. If I reject such Work and Materials or plan and schedule, I may terminate this Agreement pursuant to Paragraph 8 below.

(d) Although I will review and edit the Work and Materials, you are ultimately responsible for the accuracy and completeness of the Work and Materials, including making all changes pursuant to my review as per my instructions. Within five (5) days after I deliver review notes to you, you will make the necessary changes and provide a thorough response to any queries of questions I have communicated to you with respect thereto. If you fail to timely return the review pages, I may at my sole option (i) extend the delivery time, (ii) hire a third party to provide answers to any queries or questions unanswered by you and charge any sums due to you hereunder, or (iii) make other appropriate arrangements and proceed with my publication schedule.

4.   (a) You agree that the Work will be prepared and delivered by you as an independent contractor, and all Materials contained therein (including studio cuts and other content) and all derivative works based thereon shall be "works made for hire" (as that term is defined in the United States Copyright Law) for me. You further agree that all work for the Work will be done by you and not sub-contracted to any third parties without my prior written consent. You acknowledge that I will own all right, title and interest, including copyright and all other intellectual property and proprietary rights in and to the Materials and Work and the content contained therein and updates and revised editions thereof, throughout the world and that you will have no right, title or interest in the Materials, the Work or any derivative works based thereon, or in the copyright thereto, which shall be my sole property. To the extent such rights do not vest in me as a "work made for hire," you hereby grant, assign and transfer to me during the full term of copyright and all extensions thereof all of your right, title and interest in and to the Work and the content contained therein and all Materials contained in or prepared for the Work, and the results and proceeds thereof, throughout the universe, in all media now known or hereafter devised. I shall have the right to alter, modify or expand the Work submitted by you and to combine it with other works, to make derivative works therefrom, and to publish or not publish the Work furnished by you, at my sole discretion.

(b) You further acknowledge that I shall retain in perpetuity the sole and exclusive right to print, publish, republish, display, transmit, distribute, sell, advertise, promote and/or license the sale of the Work and the Materials, or any derivative works based thereon throughout the world in all languages and all media now known or hereinafter devised. I shall have the right, but shall not be obligated, to use your name, likeness, biographical data or professional credits on and in connection with the Work of the Work or some or all of the Material produced hereunder, or any derivative Work, and in advertising, publicity or promotion related to, and may grant such rights in connection with the license to third parties of any rights in the Work or the Materials, except as otherwise provided herein.

Work-Made-for-Hire Agreement
Contracts Companion for Writers, by Tonya M. Evans-Walls
www.LiteraryLawGuide.com

(c) You agree to execute such other assignments and instruments as I may from time to time deem necessary or desirable to evidence, establish, maintain and protect the aforementioned copyrights and all such other rights, title and interest in or to all such Material.

(d) You agree that you will not use any material contained in or produced for the Work in a work which, in my sole judgment, would be directly competitive with the Work or would be published by a direct competitor, without my prior written consent; provided that nothing herein shall prevent or preclude you from continuing to publish your own independent writings focused on the same or similar topics of sexual assault and abuse.

(e) In the course of preparing the Work and/or Materials the information provided to you, used and created by you, and that which becomes known by you in connection with your work and services for me, which includes ideas, concepts, art, audio-visual, and written and recorded materials, as well as personal, financial and business method information, is to be treated by you as my proprietary, trade secret, and confidential information. You warrant you will not discuss or use such information separate of your services rendered to me, and without my prior written approval and that you will not disclose such confidential information including the terms of this Agreement at any time during or after the term of this Agreement.

5.   The rights in the title of the Work, and any series titles, trademarks, service marks, "look and feel," and trade dress used on or in connection with the Work (hereinafter collectively referred to as the "Brand"), shall belong solely to me, and you hereby transfer and assign to me in perpetuity, any rights of ownership including without limitation copyright and/or any other intellectual property or other rights you might have therein. I shall have the exclusive right to use the Brand in all formats and media throughout the world in perpetuity or to license such rights or otherwise exploit the Brand, in any media, by itself or in arrangements with third parties, separate and apart from the Work or in combination with the Work.

6.   (a) In full and final consideration for all services you provide, and for all rights granted or relinquished by you hereunder, and upon the condition that you shall fully perform all your obligations hereunder, I shall pay you a total of $_____ (_____) as follows:

    (i) $_____ (_____) on execution of this Agreement;

    (ii) $_____ (_____) on timely delivery of the rough draft of the Work on or before [INSERT DATE] pursuant to Paragraph 2 above; and

    (iii) $_____ (_____) on timely delivery (on or before the Final Due Date) of one hundred percent (100%) of the complete Work, including the Materials, and acceptance of such Work in my sole discretion pursuant to Paragraph 2 above.

(b) Additionally, you shall receive a writer's credit on the Work and promotional materials with your name and any degree designation earned prior to publication, if requested and appropriate.

Work-Made-for-Hire Agreement
Contracts Companion for Writers, by Tonya M. Evans-Walls
www.LiteraryLawGuide.com

7.   (a) You warrant and represent the following:

(i)   You have the right to enter into this Agreement and to perform as required herein and to grant to me the rights herein granted.

(ii)   The Work has not been previously published, is wholly original, is not copied in whole or in part from any other work, except for samples from copyrighted works for which you have obtained written permission from the copyright owners at your expense on a form approved by me, and is not in the public domain.

(iii)   The Work is not (and shall not be) libelous or obscene and it does not violate the right of privacy, infringe upon or violate any copyright, trademark, trade secret or other right of any other party, or infringe any common law or statutory copyright.

(iv)   All statements asserted as fact in the Work are either true or based upon generally accepted professional research practices.

(v)   You will not use the Work or any part thereof for your own commercial, artistic or any other purposes outside of the terms of this Agreement.

(b) You agree to hold me, my licensees, representatives, agents, designees, and any seller or distributor of the Work harmless from any liability, loss or damage (including reasonable attorneys' fees) arising out of any claim, action, or proceeding which, if finally sustained or settled, would be inconsistent with or in breach of the above warranties or representations.

8.   (a) I may terminate this Agreement prior to release in the event: (i) you fail to deliver a complete, satisfactory Work pursuant to Paragraph 2 above by the due dates or fail or refuse to make the changes or edits requested in a timely manner pursuant to Paragraph 3, or (ii) Work may result in legal liability unacceptable to me in my reasonable judgment.

(b) If the Work, as revised, remains unacceptable to me for editorial reasons, you may keep the amounts paid to you in accordance with the terms set forth herein, but shall not receive the final payment due on delivery and acceptance. In the event of termination for non-delivery or for legal reasons, you shall repay to me all amounts previously paid hereunder.

(c) Upon such repayment, if any, and termination of this Agreement, my obligations to you will also terminate and all liability between the parties shall terminate. You understand and agree that I shall own all material delivered by you hereunder as well as any work in progress and I shall have the absolute rights of ownership of such material pursuant to Paragraph 4 above.

9.   (a) This Agreement sets forth the entire understanding of the parties and may not be modified except by a writing signed by both parties. This Agreement shall be construed and interpreted pursuant to the laws of the Commonwealth of Pennsylvania applicable to contracts

Work-Made-for-Hire Agreement
Contracts Companion for Writers, by Tonya M. Evans-Walls
www.LiteraryLawGuide.com

wholly entered into and performed in the Commonwealth of Pennsylvania. Any legal action, suit or proceeding arising out of or relating to this Agreement or the breach thereof shall be instituted in a court of competent jurisdiction in Philadelphia County in the Commonwealth of Pennsylvania and each party hereby consents and submits to the personal jurisdiction of such court, waives any objection to venue in such court, and consents to the service of process by registered or certified mail, return receipt requested, at the last known address of such party.

(b) This Agreement is personal to you and is not assignable without my prior written consent. This Agreement may not be modified, except in writing and signed by both parties. The provisions of paragraphs 4, 5, and 7 shall survive expiration or termination of this Agreement.

(c) You are not my employee as a result of this Agreement, and you are not entitled to any benefits (including, without limitation, pensions, medical, health, holiday or disability). You are an independent contractor and shall be solely responsible for any unemployment or disability insurance payments, or any social security, income tax or other withholdings, deductions or payments which may be required by federal, state or local law with respect to any sums paid to you hereunder. You shall indemnify and hold me harmless against any loss or damage resulting from a claim, demand, suit or proceeding brought or made against me by reason of your failure to pay the foregoing taxes or other sums.

Please sign below to confirm that this Agreement is in accordance with your understanding, and then return all copies to me for my countersignature. I will remit a fully executed copy to you for your files.

ACCEPTED AND AGREED:

By: _____   By: _____
Name: Patsi Pen   Name: Moe Doe

Social Sec. #_____   Title: _____

Date: _____   Date: _____

Citizenship: _____

Date of Birth: _____

Agency Agreement
Contracts Companion for Writers, by Tonya M. Evans-Walls
www.LiteraryLawGuide.com

SURE THING LITERARY AGENCY, LLC
AGENCY AGREEMENT

THIS AGENCY AGREEMENT ("Agreement") is entered into as of the _____ day of _____, 2007, (the "Effective Date") between _____, an individual, located at _____ (hereinafter referred to as the "Author"), and Sure Thing Literary Agency, LLC, a limited liability company whose principal place of business is located at 1234 Evergreen Terrace, Philadelphia, PA 19199 (hereinafter referred to as the "Agent"), as follows:

TERMS

1. <u>Rights; Term</u>. The Author hereby acknowledges engagement of Agent, and Agent accepts such engagement, for a term of ___ years, as of the Effective Date, as the Author's sole and exclusive agent and representative throughout the world, unless specifically limited herein, with respect to the Author's services, activities and participation in the literary publication field and the sale, lease, license or other use or disposition in any and all media now or hereafter known (hereinafter "disposition") of all book-length literary works of non-fiction and fiction, unless specifically excluded herein, (hereinafter "properties") created by the Author or owned and/or controlled by the Author or any firm or corporation owned and/or controlled by the Author. The rights herein represented by Agent include, without limitation, electronic publication, foreign publication and foreign language publication, audio recording, motion picture, television, audio-visual media, stage and all merchandising, commercial tie-up and subsidiary rights now or hereafter known relating thereto and all services rendered by the Author in connection with the exploitation of any such rights.

2. <u>Representations and Warranties</u>. The Author warrants and represents that the Author has the right to enter into this Agreement and that the Author does not have, nor will the Author hereafter enter into any agreement or incur any obligation in conflict herewith. The Agent warrants and represents that it will market the Author's properties, use its best efforts to negotiate the best available terms and conditions on Author's behalf, and use its best efforts in the foregoing for the purpose of securing deals based on the exploitation of Author's properties.

3. <u>Commission</u>.

    a. The Author agrees to pay Agent as and when received by the Author, or on the Author's behalf, or by any person, firm or corporation owned and/or controlled by the Author, directly or indirectly, or in which the Author now has or hereafter during the term hereof acquires any right, title or interest, and

Agency Agreement
Contracts Companion for Writers, by Tonya M. Evans-Walls
www.LiteraryLawGuide.com

Agent agrees to accept, as and for Agent's compensation, a sum equal to Fifteen Percent (15%) of the gross compensation and/or other consideration earned throughout the world, whether during or after the term hereof, and without deduction of any kind, pursuant to any contract negotiated during the term of this Agreement, and any and all extensions, renewals, modifications, substitutions for and additions to such contracts whenever made, and whether procured by Agent, the Author or any third party.

b. Agent shall have the right, but not the obligation, to act as packaging agent on projects involving properties and charge its customary packaging fees to third parties. Agent shall not deduct commission from the Author's compensation derived from such package if Agent actually is paid such packaging fees.

4. <u>Power of Attorney</u>. The Author agrees to authorize and direct that all payments to the Author or on the Author's behalf from engagements covered by this Agreement shall be made to and in the name of Sure Thing Literary Agency, LLC, as the Author's agent. Agent is hereby authorized (a) to collect all gross compensation and other consideration payable to the Author from engagements covered by this agreement, and (b) to endorse the Author's name to checks, drafts, choses in action and money payable in connection herewith, and deduct therefrom all commissions, loans and other monies due Agent from the Author and thereafter Agent shall remit any sums remaining as the Author shall direct within thirty (30) days of receipt and clearance of any compensation covered by this Agreement.

5. <u>Coterminous/Co-Extensive Provisions</u>.

a. The term hereof shall match the duration of and be automatically extended and re-extended with respect to any specific engagement, property or material whenever and so long as any contract or contracts covered by this Agreement (as hereinafter defined) relating to such specific engagement, property or material, shall be or continue in effect, including any and all exercises of options, extensions, renewals, modifications, substitutions for and additions to such contract(s), and for one (1) year thereafter.

b. "Contracts covered by this Agreement" means any and every agreement, oral or written, directly or indirectly related to or connected with the disposition or the refraining or the withholding from or limitation upon the disposition of any property or any part thereof or any right or interest therein, covered by this Agreement, whether procured or negotiated by Agent, the Author or any third party, whether any such agreement is now in existence or is made or negotiated or to become effective during the term hereof (or within six (6) months after each term hereof, if any such agreement is on terms similar or reasonably comparable to any offer made to the Author during the term hereof and is with the same offeror thereof or any person, firm or corporation directly or indirectly connected with such offeror); and all agreements, oral or written, substituted for or replacing

Agency Agreement
Contracts Companion for Writers, by Tonya M. Evans-Walls
www.LiteraryLawGuide.com

any such agreement, directly or indirectly, and any modifications, supplements, extensions, additions and renewals of any such agreement or substitutions or replacements thereof, whether made, negotiated or to become effective during or after the term hereof and whether procured or negotiated by Agent, the Author or any third party.

6. Non-Exclusive Agency. Agent may render similar services to others, including (a) owners of properties and/or package shows in which the Author's services, properties and/or materials are used, and (b) owners of older properties and/or materials whether or not the same as, similar to or competitive with the properties and/or materials covered by this Agreement.

7. Assignment Clause. Any assignment of any of the Author's rights covered by this Agreement shall be subject to all of Agent's rights hereunder. Agent may assign this Agreement and all of Agent's rights and obligations hereunder to a firm or corporation controlling, controlled by or under common control with Agent or to any firm or corporation affiliated with Agent or a subsidiary wholly owned by Agent.

8. Binding Contract. This Agreement shall inure to the benefit of and be binding upon Agent and the Author, the Author's heirs, and Agent's and the Author's respective successors and assigns.

9. Notice of Breach; Termination Provisions. Unless provided for elsewhere in this Agreement, no breach of this Agreement by Agent shall entitle the Author to terminate this Agreement unless within thirty (30) days after the Author learns of such breach, the Author serves written notice to Agent by certified mail, and Agent does not remedy such breach within fifteen (15) days after receipt of such notice.

10. Statement of Account; Accounting.

   a. Agent shall send copies of statements of account received by Agent to the Author when rendered.

   b. Agent shall keep the books and records with respect to payments due each party at its place of business and permit Author or Author's professional designee to inspect these books and records, at the Author's sole expense, once per year during normal business hours upon giving reasonable notice.

11. Entire Agreement. This Agreement sets forth the entire agreement between Author and Agent with respect to the subject matter hereof and this Agreement may not be modified, waived or added to except in writing signed by both parties.

12. Applicable Law. The laws of the Commonwealth of Pennsylvania shall govern this Agreement, its validity, construction and effect. Both parties agree that any conflicts regarding the terms and conditions of this contract shall be resolved by binding

Agency Agreement
Contracts Companion for Writers, by Tonya M. Evans-Walls
www.LiteraryLawGuide.com

arbitration in the Commonwealth of Pennsylvania under the rules and institutional supervision of the American Arbitration Association ("AAA"). Any decision rendered by the arbitrator may be entered in any court of any country having jurisdiction thereof. The arbitral tribunal shall consist of one neutral arbitrator appointed by the AAA. The arbitrator shall award attorney's fees to the prevailing party.

ACCEPTED AND AGREED TO:

SURE THING LITERARY AGENCY, INC.   _____, Author

By: _____   _____

Title:_____   SSN: _____

Date: _____   Date: _____

Publishing Agreement
Contracts Companion for Writers, by Tonya M. Evans-Walls
www.LiteraryLawGuide.com

PAYDAY PRESS
PUBLISHING AGREEMENT

THIS AGREEMENT is made this ___ day of _____, 20__ (The "Agreement"), by and between _____, an individual (hereinafter referred to as "Author") located at _____, and Payday Press, a Pennsylvania [sole proprietorship/partnership/limited liability company/corporation] (hereinafter referred to as "Publisher") whose principal place of business is located at _____, concerning a work presently entitled _____ (as described in greater detail below).

WHEREAS Author seeks to create a book tentatively titled _____ (the "Work");

WHEREAS Publisher seeks to publish the Work; and

WHEREAS both parties agree to be bound by the terms and conditions set forth in this Agreement,

NOW THEREFORE Author and Publisher agree as follows:

1.   Rights Granted. The Author hereby grants, transfers, and assigns to the Publisher for the full term of copyright the exclusive right to publish the Work in hardback and paperback editions (the "Primary Rights") and to sell throughout the world in all languages. The Author also grants and assigns to the Publisher the subsidiary rights (as further defined in paragraph 8 hereinbelow) to the Work, with exclusive authority to license said rights in all countries and in all languages.

2.   Delivery and Acceptance of the Manuscript.

       (a)   Author shall deliver to Publisher on or before _____, 20__ (the "Delivery Date"), one (1) original hard copy of the complete Work and one (1) copy on computer disk, together with any supplementary materials (including, without limitation, drawings, illustrations, photographs, maps, graphs, tables) as further defined in paragraph 3 hereinbelow. If Author fails to deliver the Work by the Delivery Date, after a thirty (30) day grace period (or such other time period as shall be determined by the Publisher and agreed to in writing by both parties), Publisher may demand the return of all sums paid to or on behalf of Author by Publisher in connection with the Work, and this Agreement shall terminate. Upon termination under these circumstances, Author may not resubmit the Work (or any part thereof) or a similar work to any other publisher without first offering it to Publisher under the same terms contained in this Agreement.

(b)   Publisher shall inform the Author in writing as to whether the complete Work is acceptable to Publisher in form and content within ninety (90) days of receipt of the complete Work. If Publisher determines the Work is unacceptable but capable of cure, Publisher and Author shall agree upon a time for revision (the "Revision Period") and Publisher shall provide to Author written comments explaining the necessary revisions. If Publisher determines that the first submission cannot be cured or that the revision created during the Revision Period is still unacceptable, Publisher shall have the right, in Publisher's sole discretion, to reject the Work by giving written notice to the Author. If the Work is rejected, Author shall keep fifty percent (50%) of the advances paid to date and shall return the remaining fifty percent (50%) within one year of rejection. The Author may submit the Work to a third party, provided that Author shall remain obligated to repay to Publisher the amounts retained by Author from all proceeds from any sale or license by the Author of rights of any nature in the Work to a third party (the "First Proceeds").

3.   Supplementary Material.

(a)   The Author will prepare, or cause to be prepared, and deliver to the Publisher within ___ weeks of the receipt of page proofs an index to the Work acceptable to the Publisher at the Author's own expense, unless the parties agree that an index will not be needed.

(b)   If permissions to use copyrighted work in the Work are necessary, the Author shall obtain such permissions at the Author's own expense (after consultation with the Publisher) and shall file them with the Publisher at the time the manuscript is delivered (or as agreed to prior to Delivery) in form and substance satisfactory to Publisher, in Publisher's sole discretion. [Include only if permissions are necessary: Publisher acknowledges that the permissions request form attached hereto as Exhibit A shall be sufficient evidence, when fully and properly executed, of permission.]

4.   Representations and Warranties.

(a)   The Author warrants that he/she is the sole owner of the Work and has full power and authority to make this Agreement, [that the Work is fictional,] and that the Work does not infringe the copyright in any other work, violate the rights to privacy or publicity of any person, or constitute a defamation against any person or entity.

(b)   Publisher represents and warrants that it is a company duly organized, validly existing, and in good standing under the laws of its jurisdiction of charter, having all requisite power and authority to enter into this Agreement, and that it will make no additions or changes to the Work that infringe the copyright in any other work, violate the rights to privacy or publicity of any person, or constitute a defamation against any person or entity.

5.   Duty to Publish.

(a)   The Work shall be published by the Publisher in the English language as soon as circumstances permit after acceptance of the completed manuscript, but in no event later than eighteen (18) months after acceptance, at its own expense, in such style or styles and at such price or prices as the Publisher shall deem best suited to the sale of the Work. Notwithstanding the foregoing, Publisher's inadvertent failure to exploit the Work, including Author's non-performance or by reason of Force Majeure (which shall include, without limitation, any event which Publisher could not foresee, such as fire, flood or other natural disasters, acts of God, acts of a public enemy or terrorist, Internet failures, governmental or court order, national emergency, strikes or labor disputes, the effect of which Publisher could not prevent or predict and which renders impossible or impractical the performance of contractual obligations either totally or in part), shall not be deemed a breach hereof.

(b)   The Author will bear the expense of any alterations made in the proofs by the Author (exclusive of printer's or Publisher's staff errors) which exceed ten percent (10%) of the cost of the composition.

6.   Artistic Control. The Publisher [, in consultation with the Author,] shall make all artistic decisions.

7.   Royalties. The Publisher shall pay to the Author on each copy of the Work sold by the Publisher, the following royalties based on the Net Sales of the Work ("Net Sales" being defined as sales, less returns, at list price less trade discounts):

[(a)   Hardback: Ten percent (10%) on the first 5,000 copies; twelve and one-half percent (12 ½%) on the next 5,000 copies; fifteen percent (15%) on all copies thereafter.]

(b)   Paperback: Seven and one-half (7 ½%) on the first 10,000 copies; 10% on all copies thereafter.

[(c)   Mass Market: Six percent (6%) on the first 150,000 copies; eight percent (8%) on all copies thereafter.]

(d)   On all copies sold at special discount of 60% or more from the list price, a royalty of ten percent (10%) of the amount the Publisher receives, except as provided in paragraph 16.

(e)   On copies sold for export (outside the United States and Canada), fifty percent (50%) of the royalties stipulated in paragraphs [7(a) - (c)], except as provided in paragraph 16.

(f)   No royalty shall be paid on copies furnished without charge for review, advertising, sample, promotion or other similar purposes, or on damaged copies or Author copies.

8.   Performance Bonuses.

(a)   In addition to the advance and royalties payable under this Agreement and subject to the limits stated in 8(a)(vii) and 8(d) hereinbelow, the Publisher shall pay to the Author bonuses as additional advances against royalties (individually a "Bestseller Bonus" and collectively the "Bestseller Bonuses") as follows:

(i)   For each week the Work appears on The New York Times Bestseller list in a position no less than first (1st) and no greater than fifth (5th) on the list, the Publisher shall pay to the Author, as an additional advance against royalties, a Bestseller Bonus of $_____. Publisher shall make any such payments within thirty (30) days of any qualifying appearance.

(ii)   For each week the Work appears on The New York Times Bestseller list in a position no less than sixth (6th) and no greater than tenth (10th) on the list, the Publisher shall pay to the Author, as an additional advance against royalties, a Bestseller Bonus of $_____. Publisher shall make any such payments within thirty (30) days of any qualifying appearance.

(iii) For each week the Work appears on the New York Times Bestseller list in a position no less than eleventh (11th) and no greater than fifteenth (15th) on the list, the Publisher shall pay to the Author, as an additional advance against royalties, a Bestseller Bonus of $_____. Publisher shall make any such payments within thirty (30) days of any qualifying appearance.

(iv) For each week the Work appears on the USA Today Bestseller list in a position no less than first (1st) and no greater than fifteenth (15th) on the list, the Publisher shall pay to the Author, as an additional advance against royalties, a Bestseller Bonus of $_____. Publisher shall make any such payments within thirty (30) days of any qualifying appearance.

(v) For each week the Work appears on the USA today Bestseller list in a position no less than sixteenth (16th) and no greater than twenty-fifth (25th) on such list, the Publisher shall pay to the Author, as an additional advance against royalties, a Bestseller Bonus of $_____. Publisher shall make any such payments within thirty (30) days of any qualifying appearance.

(vi) If the Publisher pays a Bestseller Bonus or any combination of Bestseller Bonuses to the Author, and such payment subsequently results in an overpayment of royalties, then the Publisher shall be entitled to recoup such overpayments from all monies due and payable on account of the Work.

(vii) Anything to the contrary notwithstanding, the maximum Bestseller Bonus payable to the Author pursuant to this Subparagraph 8(a) shall be $_____.

(b)   In addition to the advance and royalties payable under this Agreement, the Publisher shall pay to the Author, as an additional advance against royalties, the following bonus based upon the sales performance of the trade paperback edition of the Work (the "Performance Bonus"). Accordingly if the Publisher distributes 50,000 copies or more of the Work trade paperback edition of the Work, and if such trade paperback book has a sell-through (as the term is commonly understood in the publishing and bookselling industry) of 80% or higher at the rendering of royalty statement not less than twelve (12) months and not more than eighteen (18) months after the official publication date of such edition, the publisher shall pay the author as an additional advance against royalties, the sum of $_____.

(c)   In addition to the advance of royalties payable under this Agreement, the Publisher shall pay to the Author, as an additional advance against royalties, (individually an "Essence Magazine Bonus" and collectively as "Essence Magazine Bonuses"), as follows:

(i) For each month the Work appears on Essence magazines bestseller list in a position of first (1st) on the list, the Publisher shall pay to the Author, as and additional advance against royalties, a Bonus of $_____. Publisher shall make any such payment within thirty (30) days of any qualifying appearance.

(ii) For each month the work appears on Essence magazines bestseller list in a position no less than second (2nd) and no greater than fifth (5th) on the list, the Publisher shall pay to the Author, as an additional advance against royalties, a Bonus of $_____. Publisher shall make any such payment within thirty (30) days of any qualifying appearance.

(iii) If Publisher pays a Essence Magazine Bonus or any combination of Essence Magazine Bonuses to the Author, and such payments subsequently results in an overpayment of royalties, then the Publisher shall be entitled to recoup such overpayments from all monies due and payable on account of the Work.

(iv) Anything to the contrary not withstanding, the maximum Essence Magazine Bonus payable to the author hereunder shall be $_____.

(d)   The maximum bestseller bonus amount payable by the Publisher under the terms of Subparagraphs (a) and (c) hereinabove shall be $_____ for the Work, and it is understood and agreed that all bonuses paid by Publisher to Author under the terms of this Paragraph 8 shall be considered and accounted for as additional advances against royalties.

9.   Subsidiary Rights.   The Publisher shall have the sole right to license, sell, or otherwise dispose of the following rights in the Work: publication or sale by book clubs; reprint rights; foreign rights; translation rights; publication in anthologies, compilations, digests, condensations; first and second serial rights (in one or more installments); dramatic, motion picture, and television rights; broadcast by radio; recordings; electronic (including Internet), audio, mechanical, and visual reproduction; computer programs; microprint, microfiche, and microfilm editions; syndication rights; permission rights (quotations, excerpts, illustrations, etc.); any other rights subsidiary to the Work not specifically enumerated and in any media now known or hereafter created; and otherwise utilize the Work and material based on the Work.

10.   Accounting and Payments.

    (a)   The Publisher shall render to the Author in June and December of each year a biannual statement of account that covers the preceding six (6) month period, which shall signal the close of the preceding accounting period. The statement shall show for that period and cumulatively to date the number of copies: (i) printed and bound, (ii) sold and returned for each royalty rate, (iii) distributed free for publicity purposes, (iv) remaindered, destroyed, or lost, (v) the royalties paid to and owed to the Author, (vi) licensing income, and (vii) the Publisher's reserve against returns, if any. Payment shall be made within thirty (30) days of the close of the applicable accounting period in US dollars. If the Publisher sets up a reserve against returns of books, it shall in not exceed fifteen percent (15%) of royalties due to the Author in any period.

    (b)   If any payments due to Author are in arrears for more than two accounting periods, Author shall have the right to demand immediate payment within thirty (30) days of all outstanding sums due. If payment is not made within such thirty day time period, all rights granted hereunder shall revert automatically back to Author and all legal and equitable remedies shall be preserved.

[NOTE: This provision is particularly important with small/independent publishers.]

11.   Inspection of Books.   Author, along with Author's legal or financial representative, shall, upon giving written notice to Publisher or Publisher's designee, have the right once per year to inspect the Publisher's books of account to verify the accounting. If errors in any such accounting are found to be to the Author's disadvantage and represent more than ten percent (10%) of the payment to the Author pursuant to said accounting, and Author notifies Publisher of such within thirty (30) days after completing the audio, the cost of the accounting shall be paid by the Publisher. In that case, such payments owed to Author shall be payable within ninety (90) days of Publisher's receipt of notice of accounting error.

12.   Copyright. Publisher shall in all versions of the Work published by Publisher under this Agreement, place a notice of copyright in the name of the author (ex: © 200__

by _____) in a form and place that Publisher reasonably believes to comply with the requirements of the United States copyright law, and shall apply for registration of such copyright(s) in the name of the Author in the United States Copyright Office. Publisher shall have the right, but not the obligation, to apply for registration of copyright(s) in the Work published by Publisher elsewhere in the world. Author shall execute and deliver to Publisher any and all documents which Publisher deems necessary or appropriate to evidence or effectuate the rights granted in this Agreement, including but not limited to the Instrument of Recordation. Nothing contained in this Section shall be construed as limiting, modifying or otherwise affecting any of the rights granted to Publisher under this Agreement.

13.   Indemnity. Author and Publisher (each an "Indemnifying Party") hereby agree to indemnify and hold each other harmless from and against any and all claims, demands, actions and rights of action (including reasonable attorneys' fees and costs) which shall or may arise by virtue of: (i) anything done or omitted to be done by the Indemnifying Party (through or by his agents, employees or other representatives) outside the scope of, or in breach of the terms of, this Agreement; (ii) any breach of warranty or representation contained herein; and (iii) any misrepresentation, omission or inaccuracy in any schedule, instrument or paper delivered or to be delivered hereunder or in connection with the transaction herein contemplated.

14.   Author Copies. The Publisher shall give to the Author, free of charge, twenty-five (25) copies of each edition of the Work as published. Author may purchase additional copies from Publisher [for personal use (not for resale)] at the Publisher's best available discount at the time of purchase, without royalty to the Author. Publisher may deduct the cost of said additional copies from Author's account in lieu of actual payment by Author for such copies.

15.   Out-of-Print, Reversion.

        (a)   If the work goes out of print in all Publisher's editions (including electronic as further defined hereinbelow), Author shall have the right to request that Publisher reprint or cause a licensee to reprint the Work. Publisher shall have six (6) months after receipt of any such written request from Author to comply, unless prevented from doing so by circumstances beyond Publisher's control. If Publisher declines to reprint the work as described above or if Publisher agrees to reprint the work but fails to do so within the time allowed to do so, then Author may terminate this Agreement upon thirty (30) days' written notice. Upon such termination, all rights granted under this Agreement, except the rights to dispose of existing copies as set forth in paragraph 16 below, shall revert to Author, subject to all rights which may have been granted by Publisher to third parties under this Agreement, and Publisher shall have no further obligations or liabilities to Author except that Author's earned royalties shall be paid when and as due. Except as provided elsewhere in this Agreement, the work shall not be deemed out of print within the meaning of this section so long as the work is available for sale either from stock in Publisher's, a distributor's or a licensees' warehouse, or in regular sales channels.

(b)   If Publisher sells no more than [twenty-five (25)] copies of Author's Work in either electronic or downloadable format, or by means of print-on-demand technology, over any twelve (12) consecutive month period of this Agreement, then the work shall be deemed out-of-print as to such editions and, if all other editions are also deemed out-of-print, either party may terminate this Agreement upon thirty (30) days' written notice sent to the other party. Upon such termination, all rights granted under this Agreement, except the rights to dispose of existing copies, if applicable, including but not limited to electronic, printed, or audio copies, shall revert to Author, subject to all rights that may have been granted by Publisher to third parties under this Agreement, and Publisher shall have no further obligations or liabilities to Author except that Author's earned royalties shall be paid when and as due.

16.   Remaindering. If Publisher shall determine that there is insufficient demand for the Work to enable the Publisher to continue its publication and sale profitably, the Publisher may dispose of the copies remaining on hand as it deems best. In such event, Author shall have the right, within thirty (30) days of receiving written notice from Publisher (Notice of Intent to Remainder), to a single purchase of some or all of such copies at the best available discount, and the purchase of printer files, film and/or plates, as applicable, at Publisher's actual cost of manufacture. If Author declines to purchase such copies, Publisher may dispose of them and shall pay Author a sum equal to ten percent (10%) of the amounts actually received by Publisher.

17.   Promotion of the Work. The Publisher may publish or permit others to publish or broadcast without charge and without royalty such excerpts from the Work for publicity purposes as may benefit the sale of the Work. Further, the Author consents to the use of his/her name and likeness to promote and advertise the Work.

18.   No-Compete Clause. The Author agrees not to publish or furnish to any other publisher, without the Publisher's written consent, during the term of this Agreement any work on the same subject and of the same content and character as the Work covered by this Agreement, publication of which would, in the Publisher's opinion, clearly conflict with the sale of the Work.

19.   Options Clause. The Publisher shall, within one hundred eighty (180) days from the date of publication, have the option to acquire Author's next book-length work of [insert genre] on the same terms has set forth hereunder [Alternate provision for authors with sufficient value to the company: on terms to be mutually agreed upon by the parties.]

20.   Amendments. The written provisions contained in this Agreement constitute the sole and entire agreement made between the Author and the Publisher concerning this Work and any amendments to this Agreement shall not be valid unless made in writing and signed by both parties.

21.   <u>Notice Provisions</u>. Where written notice is required hereunder, such notice, as well as royalty statements and copies of payments to be made hereunder, shall be given or made to the respective party at the addresses in the introductory paragraph.

A copy of all notices to Author shall also be sent to:

Author's Agent:
Company
Address
Phone:
Fax:
Email:

Author's Attorney:
Firm
Address
Phone:
Fax:
Email:

22.   <u>Construction, Governing Law, Binding Effect, and Assignment</u>. This Agreement shall be construed and interpreted according to the laws of the Commonwealth of Pennsylvania and shall be binding upon the parties hereto, their heirs, successors, assigns, and personal representatives. All claims, disputes or disagreements which may arise out of the interpretation, performance or breach of this Agreement shall be submitted exclusively to the jurisdiction and venue of the Commonwealth of Pennsylvania. Each of the parties to this Agreement consent to the exclusive personal jurisdiction and venue of the courts, state and federal, that are located in Philadelphia County, Pennsylvania.

[NOTE: Also consider a binding Arbitration provision instead of litigation or in addition to for lesser controversies.]

23.   <u>Waiver; Invalidity</u>. The waiver by either party of any breach of this Agreement in any one or more instances shall in no way be construed as a waiver of any subsequent breach of this Agreement (whether or not similar in nature). If any part of this Agreement shall be held to be void, invalid or unenforceable, it shall not affect the validity of the balance of this Agreement.

24.   <u>Unique Services</u>. Author acknowledges that the services rendered hereunder are of a special, unique, unusual, extraordinary, and intellectual character which gives them a particular value, the loss of which cannot be reasonably or adequately compensated in damages in any action at law, and that a breach by the Author of any of the provisions of this Agreement will cause Publisher great and irreparable injury and damage. Author expressly agrees that Publisher shall be entitled to the remedies of injunction and other equitable relief to prevent a breach of this Agreement or any provision hereof and said relief shall be in addition to any other remedies for damages or otherwise, which shall be available to the Publisher.

25.   <u>Legal Counsel</u>. Writer hereby warrants and represents that Writer has been advised of Writer's right to seek legal counsel of Writer's own choosing in connection with the negotiation and execution of this Agreement, and that Writer has had the opportunity to confer with such counsel prior to the execution hereof. Further, neither Publisher nor any of its principals have acted as legal counsel on behalf of Writer in regard to this Agreement.

26.   <u>Entire Agreement</u>. This represents the entire agreement between the parties. All modifications must be in writing and signed by both parties.

IN WITNESS WHEREOF, the parties have duly executed this Agreement as of the date first written above.

PAYDAY PRESS   AUTHOR

By:_____   _____
       Authorized signatory   [_____]

_____   _____
Title/Position   Address

                                     _____
                                     City, State Zip

                                     _____
                                     Social Security Number

Single Songwriting Agreement
Contracts Companion for Writers, by Tonya M. Evans-Walls
www.LiteraryLawGuide.com

SINGLE SONGWRITING AGREEMENT

THIS AGREEMENT is made and entered into this _____day of _____,2007 (the "Effective Date"), by and between **Starz Publishing Company, LLC,** of 987 Superstar Way, Suite 1000, Philadelphia, Pennsylvania, (hereinafter referred to as "Publisher"), and _____, of _____, (hereinafter individually referred to as "Writer").

FOR AND IN CONSIDERATION OF the mutual covenants set forth, the parties do hereby agree as follows:

1.   **Grant of Rights:** The Writer hereby sells, assigns, transfers and delivers to the Publisher, its successors and assigns, the original musical composition written and composed by Writer (the "Work") presently titled _____, which title may be changed by the Publisher; including the title, words and music thereof, and all rights therein, and all copyright and the right to secure copyrights and any extensions and renewals of copyright in the same and in any arrangements and adaptations thereof, throughout the world; and any and all other rights that the Writer now has or to which Writer may be entitled or hereafter could or might secure with respect to the Work throughout the world; and to have and to hold the same absolutely unto the Publisher its successors and assigns. Writer acknowledges that included within the rights and interests hereinabove referred to, without limitation, is Writer's irrevocable grant to Publisher, its successors, licensees, sub-licensees and assigns, of the sole and exclusive right, license, privilege, and authority throughout the entire world with respect to the Work as follows:

(a)   To perform, or cause to be performed, the Work publicly, whether for profit or otherwise, by means of public or private performance, radio or Internet broadcasting, television, or by any and all means, whether now known or which may hereafter come into existence;

(b)   To substitute a new title or titles for the Work and to make any arrangement, adaptation, translation, dramatization or transcription of the Work, in whole or part, and in connection with any other literary, musical or dramatic material, and (except as otherwise provided in an addendum hereto) to add new lyrics to the music of the Work or new music to the lyrics of the Work, all as Publisher may deem expedient or desirable. In the event Publisher is directly involved in the printing of sheet music containing the Work, Publisher agrees to make all reasonable efforts to produce a reproduction of Writer's original recording of the Work as accurately as possible; provided that any inadvertent failure of the Publisher to do so shall not be deemed a material breach of Publisher's obligations hereunder.

Single Songwriting Agreement
Contracts Companion for Writers, by Tonya M. Evans-Walls
www.LiteraryLawGuide.com

(c) To secure copyright registration and protection of the Work in Publisher's name or otherwise as Publisher may desire at Publisher's own cost and expense and at Publisher's election, including any and all renewals and extensions of copyright, and to have and to hold said copyright, renewals, extensions and all rights of whatsoever nature thereunder existing, for and during the full term of said copyright and all renewals and extensions thereof;

(d) To make or cause to be made, and to license others to make, master records, transcriptions, sound tracks, pressings, and any other mechanical, electrical or other productions of the Work, in whole or part, in such form or manner and as frequently as Publisher, in Publisher's sole and uncontrolled discretion, shall determine, including the right to synchronize the same with sound motion pictures, and the right to manufacture, advertise, license or sell such reproductions for any and all purposes, including, without limitation, private performances and public performances, radio and Internet broadcasts, television, sound motion pictures, wired radio or cable television, phonographs, and any and all other means or devices whether now known or which may hereafter come into existence;

(e) To print, publish and sell, and to license others to print, publish and sell, sheet music, orchestrations, arrangements and other editions of the Work in all forms, including, without limitation, the inclusion of any or all of the Work in song folios, song books, mixed or lyric magazines with or without music; and

(f) Any and all other rights of every and any nature now known or hereafter existing by virtue of any common law and statutory rights and copyrights and renewals and extensions thereof in the Work. Writer grants Publisher, without any compensation other than as specified herein, the perpetual right to use and to publish, and to permit others to use and publish, Writer's name (including any professional name heretofore or hereafter adopted by Writer), Writer's photograph or any other likeness, which shall be approved by Writer, Writer's logos and trademarks whether now in existence or created after the Effective Date hereof or during any period of time Publisher controls the rights granted to it herein, biographical material concerning Writer, and the titles of the Work, in connection with the printing, sale, advertising, performance, distribution and other exploitation of the Work hereunder, and for any other purpose related to the music business of Publisher, its affiliated and related companies, or the refrain therefrom.

2. **Warranties, Representations, Covenants and Agreements**: Writer hereby warrants, represents, covenants and agrees as follows:

(a) Writer has the full right, power and authority to enter into and perform this Agreement and to grant to and vest in Publisher all the rights herein set forth, free and clear of any and all claims, rights and obligations whatsoever;

Single Songwriting Agreement
Contracts Companion for Writers, by Tonya M. Evans-Walls
www.LiteraryLawGuide.com

(b)   The Work, including the title, lyrics and music thereof, and each and every part thereof, delivered by Writer hereunder, is new and original and capable of copyright protections throughout the entire world;

(c)   The Work is not an imitation or copy of, or infringes upon any other material, or violates or infringes upon any common law or statutory rights of any kind including without limitation, contractual rights, intellectual property rights, and rights of privacy, and publicity, and

(d)   Writer has not sold, assigned, leased, licensed or in any way disposed of or encumbered the Work or rights herein granted to Publisher, and shall not sell, assign, lease, license or in any other way dispose of or encumber the Work or said rights.

3.   **Power of Attorney**: Writer does hereby irrevocably constitute, authorize, empower and appoint Publisher, or any of its officers, assignees, licensees or designees, as Writer's true and lawful agent (with full power of substitution and delegation), to enter into contracts in Writer's name, and in Writer's place and stead, or in Publisher's name, and to take and do such action, and to make, sign, execute, acknowledge and deliver all instruments or documents, which Publisher, or its, successors, assignees, licensees, or designees deems desirable or necessary to secure all of the rights or interests granted by Writer hereunder, including, without limitation, such documents as Publisher may deem desirable or necessary to secure for Publisher or its successors, assignees, licensees, or designees and Writer or its successors, assignees, licensees, or designees the worldwide copyright for the Work for the entire term of copyright and for any and all renewals and extensions thereof.

4.   **Consideration**: In consideration of this Agreement, the Publisher agrees to pay the Writer as follows:

(a)   Fifty percent (50%) of any and all Net Sums (as hereinafter defined) actually received by Publisher from sales, licenses and other uses of the Work (other than public performance royalties as herein mentioned in subsection (c) below) by Publisher or its subsidiary, assignee, licensee, or designee, throughout the Territory pursuant to this Agreement, including without limitation, regular piano copies and dance orchestration or other arrangements (ex: song folios, song books), mechanical rights, electrical transcription and reproduction rights, electronic rights, motion picture, television, and all other audiovisual works, product and advertising synchronization rights and all other rights therein, for which payment has been received by Publisher in the United States. The term "Net Sums" is defined as gross sums less any and all reasonable costs and expenses including, without limitation, advances or other payments to Writer, copyright registration fees, administration expenses (including general overhead), actual and reasonable out-of-pocket third party audit and legal fees, promotional costs, and other recoupable expenses.

(b)   Writer shall receive his public performance royalties throughout the world directly from the performing rights society to which he is affiliated (i.e., ASCAP,

Single Songwriting Agreement
Contracts Companion for Writers, by Tonya M. Evans-Walls
www.LiteraryLawGuide.com

BMI, or SESAC) and shall not have any claim whatsoever against Publisher for any sums received by Publisher from any performing rights society which makes payments directly (or indirectly other than through the Publisher) to writers, authors and composers.

(c) Publisher shall not be required to pay any sums on professional or complimentary copies or any copies of musical derivatives of the Work which are distributed gratuitously to performing artists, orchestra leaders and disc jockeys or for advertising, promotional or exploitation purposes. Furthermore, no royalties shall be payable to Writer for consigned copies of the Work unless paid for, and not until such time as an accounting therefore can be properly made.

(d) Payments as hereinabove specified shall be payable solely to Writer if Writer is the sole author of the Work, including the words and music thereof. However, in the event that one or more other songwriters are authors together with Writer of the Work (including songwriters employed by Publisher, in Publisher's sole discretion, to add, change, or translate the words or to revise or change the music), the foregoing royalties shall be divided between or among Writer and the other songwriters as per the terms and conditions stated in 4(e) hereinbelow.

(e) Writer agrees that the foregoing royalties (and fifty percent (50%) of the publisher's share) payable hereunder to the Writer and any coauthors of the Work shall be divided amongst Writer and such coauthors and paid in accordance with the following percentages:

Name: _____   Percentage: _____

Name: _____   Percentage: _____

Name: _____   Percentage: _____

Name: _____   Percentage: _____

Name: _____   Percentage: _____

(f) Except as herein expressly provided, no other royalties or monies shall be paid to Writer.

5. **Accounting**: Writer shall receive accountings and payments from Publisher on a semi-annual basis within thirty (30) days after Publisher's actual receipt of such accountings and payments in the United States. No payments shall become payable to Writer under this Agreement until such payment has been actually received by Publisher from its assignees, licensees, or designees. Writer shall have the right, through a Certified Public Accountant or attorney, to inspect Publisher's books and records, in pertinent part as the same relates to the computation of Writer's royalties hereunder, provided such inspection shall only occur once per year after Writer has given Publisher thirty (30) days written notice. If no objection is received to an accounting statement made hereunder within two (2) years from the date of its submission to Writer, Writer shall be deemed to have waived any right to object to such statement.

Single Songwriter Agreement   **5 of 7**

Single Songwriting Agreement
Contracts Companion for Writers, by Tonya M. Evans-Walls
www.LiteraryLawGuide.com

6.   **Duty to Publish**: The Publisher agrees to publish, or cause to be published, the Work, within one (1) year after delivery and acceptance. Should Publisher fail to do so, the Writer shall have the right, by giving written notice, as provided for in Paragraph 11 hereinbelow, to demand the return of the Work, whereupon the Publisher must, within sixty (60) days after receipt of such notice, either publish the Work, in which event this Agreement shall remain in full force and effect as to the Work; provided that if Publisher has entered into negotiations to publish the Work, or Publisher (or Publisher's production or recording designee) has entered into negotiations with a prospective Distributor prior to the expiration of the sixty (60) day period, Publisher shall have an additional period of nine (9) months to consummate such agreement (the "Negotiation Period"). If such agreement has been consummated, then this Agreement shall remain in full force. If after the expiration of the Negotiation Period Publisher has not consummated such agreement, all rights of any and every nature granted to the Publisher herein in connection with the Work shall revert to and become the property of the Writer and shall be reassigned to Writer. Without limiting the foregoing, Writer understands and agrees that if the Publisher shall secure a commercial recording, or an electrical transcription, or a synchronization in a motion picture of a Work, such recording, transcription or synchronization shall, for the purposes of this Agreement, be deemed publication by the Publisher or its designee.

7.   **Assignment**: Publisher may assign this Agreement or delegate Publisher's responsibilities assumed hereunder, at the Publisher's sole discretion, to any subsidiary, affiliated or controlling company or to any other assignee, licensee or designee, provided that such assignment or license shall not relieve Publisher of its obligations under this Agreement. Writer may not assign or delegate any rights or obligations hereunder (except the right to receive payments) without the prior written approval of the Publisher.

8.   **Legal Actions**: Publisher may take such action as it deems necessary, either in Writer's name or in its own name, against any person or entity to protect all rights and interests acquired by Publisher hereunder. Writer will, at Publisher's request, cooperate fully with Publisher in any controversy which may arise or litigation which may be brought concerning Publisher's rights and interests obtained hereunder. Publisher shall have the right, in its absolute discretion, to employ attorneys and to institute or defend any action or proceeding and to take any other proper steps to protect the right, title and interest of Publisher in and to the Work. Publisher shall also have the right, in its sole discretion, to settle, compromise or in any other manner dispose of any matter, claim, action or proceeding and to satisfy any judgment that may be rendered in an action brought by Publisher against any alleged infringer of the Work. After deducting the expense of litigation, including without limitation attorney's fees and court costs, Publisher shall pay to Writer a sum equal to fifty percent (50%) of such net proceeds. Writer agrees to, and does hereby, indemnify, save and hold Publisher harmless from any and all loss connected with any claim by a third party which is inconsistent with any covenant, representation or warranty made by Writer in this Agreement, and Writer agrees to reimburse Publisher, on demand, with respect to any liability or claim to which the foregoing indemnity applies. Pending the determination of any such claim, Publisher may withhold payments otherwise due to Writer as a reserve.

9.   **Definitions**: For purposes of this Agreement, the word "person" means and refers to any individual, company, partnership, association or any other organized group of persons, or the legal successors or representatives of the foregoing. Whenever the expressions "the term of this

Single Songwriting Agreement
Contracts Companion for Writers, by Tonya M. Evans-Walls
www.LiteraryLawGuide.com

Agreement" or "period" or words of similar connotation are included herein, they shall be deemed to mean and refer to the initial term of this Agreement and any and all renewals, extensions, substitutions or replacements of this Agreement, whether expressly indicated or otherwise. Where more than one person shall comprise Writer, the singular shall also include the plural, as applicable.

10.   **Modification, Waiver, Invalidity and Controlling Law**: This Agreement shall supersede any other agreements previously entered into by the parties which affect any rights and obligations herein to the extent that such other agreements grant lesser rights to Publisher in and to the Work. Further, this Agreement may not be canceled, altered, modified, amended or waived, in whole or in part, in any way, except by instrument in writing signed by the parties. The waiver by either party of any breach of this Agreement in any one or more instances shall in no way be construed as a waiver of any subsequent breach of this Agreement (whether or not similar in nature). If any part of this Agreement shall be held to be void, invalid or unenforceable, it shall not affect the validity of the balance of this Agreement. This Agreement shall be deemed to have been made in the Commonwealth of Pennsylvania, and its validity, construction and effect shall be governed by the laws of the Commonwealth of Pennsylvania applicable to agreements wholly performed therein. This Agreement shall not be binding upon Publisher until fully executed by Writer.

11.   **Notices**: All important notices (other than statements of account pursuant to Paragraph 5 hereinabove) between the parties must be submitted by Certified Mail, return receipt requested, or other verifiable means of delivery, to the last known address of the applicable party to this Agreement, and a copy of such notice shall be sent to the legal representative of such party, if known or previously disclosed by the receiving party.

12.   **Miscellaneous**: The headings set forth in this Agreement are solely for the sake of convenience and shall not be deemed to restrict or limit the scope of any provision herein. Additionally, this Agreement may be executed in counterparts.

13.   **Right to Independent Legal Representation**: Each party to this Agreement warrants that such party has read and understands the terms herein. Writer acknowledges that he was advised to seek independent legal counsel in connection with the negotiation hereof prior to executing this Agreement and whether or not Writer has done so, Writer hereby waives any right Writer might otherwise have to challenge the validity of this Agreement based on Writer's failure to understand its terms.

(Signature page follows)

Single Songwriting Agreement
Contracts Companion for Writers, by Tonya M. Evans-Walls
www.LiteraryLawGuide.com

IN WITNESS WHEREOF, the parties hereto have executed this Agreement as of the date and year above written.

By: STARZ PUBLISHING COMPANY, LLC

_____
Signatory

_____
Title/Position

_____
Address

_____
City, State Zip

_____
Writer

_____
Social Security Number

_____
Writer

_____
Social Security Number

Exclusive Songwriter Agreement
Contracts Companion for Writers, by Tonya M. Evans-Walls
www.LiteraryLawGuide.com

SONGWRITER'S AND COMPOSER'S AGREEMENT

THIS AGREEMENT made and entered into this day of January 1, 20__ by and between _____ (hereinafter referred to as "Publisher") and _____, _____ and _____ (hereinafter collectively referred to as "Writer").

1. <u>Employment</u>. Publisher hereby employs Writer to render his services as a songwriter and composer and otherwise as may be hereinafter set forth. Writer hereby accepts such employment and agrees to render such services exclusively for Publisher during the term hereof, upon the terms and conditions set forth herein.

2. <u>Term</u>. The term of this Agreement shall commence with the date hereof and shall continue in force for a period of _____ from said date (the "Term"). Writer hereby grants to Publisher _____ separate and irrevocable options each to extend this Agreement for a one (1) year term, such extension terms to run consecutively beginning at the expiration of the original term hereof, all upon the same terms and conditions as are applicable to the initial term (and collectively referred to as the "Term"). Each option shall be automatically exercised unless written notice to the contrary is sent by Publisher to Writer at least ten (10) days prior to the expiration of the then current term. Such notice to the contrary may, at Publisher's election, be effective as to individual members of Writer or as to all members of Writer.

3. <u>Grant of Rights</u>. Writer hereby irrevocably and absolutely assigns, transfers, sets over and grants to Publisher its successors and assigns each and every and all rights and interests of every kind, nature and description in and to the results and proceeds of Writer's services hereunder, including but not limited to the titles, words and music of any and all original musical compositions in any and all forms and original arrangements of musical compositions in the public domain in any and all forms, and/or all rights and interests existing under all agreements and licenses relating thereto, together with all worldwide copyrights and renewals and extensions thereof, which musical works have been written, composed, created or conceived, in whole or part, by Writer alone or in collaboration with another or others, and which may hereafter, during the Term hereof, be written, composed, created or conceived by Writer, in whole or in part, alone or in collaboration with another or others, and which are now owned or controlled and which may, during the Term hereof, be owned or controlled, directly or indirectly, by Writer, alone or with others, or as the employer of transferee, directly or indirectly, of the writers or composers thereof, including the title, words and music of each such composition, and all worldwide copyrights and renewals and extensions thereof, all of which Writer does hereby represent are and shall at all times be Publisher's sole and exclusive property as the sole owner thereof, free from any adverse claims or rights therein by any other person, firm or corporation.

Writer acknowledges that, included within the rights and interests hereinabove referred to, but without limiting the generality of the foregoing, is Writer's irrevocable grant to Publisher, its successors, licensees, sublicensees and assigns, of the sole and exclusive right, license, privilege

Exclusive Songwriter Agreement
Contracts Companion for Writers, by Tonya M. Evans-Walls
www.LiteraryLawGuide.com

and authority (but not the obligation) throughout the entire world with respect to the said original musical compositions and original arrangements of compositions in the public domain, whether now in existence or hereafter created during the Term hereof, as follows:

(a) To perform said musical compositions publicly for profit by means of public and private performance, radio broadcasting, television, or any and all other means, whether now known or which may hereafter come into existence.

(b) To substitute a new title or titles for said compositions and to make any arrangement, adaptation, translation, dramatization and transposition of said composition, in whole or in part, and in connection with any other musical, literary or dramatic material, and to add new lyrics to the music of said compositions or new music to the lyrics of said compositions, all as Publisher may deem expedient or desirable.

(c) To secure copyright registration and protection of said compositions in Publisher's name or otherwise as Publisher may desire at Publisher's own cost and expense and at Publisher's election, including any and all renewals and extensions of copyrights, and to have and to hold said copyrights, renewals, extensions and all rights of whatsoever nature thereunder existing, for and during the full term of all said copyrights and all renewals and extensions thereof.

(d) To make or cause to be made, master records, transcriptions, sound tracks, pressings, and any other mechanical, electrical or other reproductions of said compositions, in whole or in part, in such form or manner and as frequently as Publisher's sole and uncontrolled discretion shall determine, including the right to synchronize the same with sound motion pictures and the right to manufacture, advertise, license or sell such reproductions for any and all purposes, including but not limited to private performances and public performances, by broadcasting, television, sound motion pictures, wired radio and any and all other means or devices whether now known or which may hereafter come into existence.

(e) To print, publish and sell sheet music, orchestrations, arrangements and other editions of the said compositions in all forms, including the right to include any or all of said compositions in song folios or lyric magazines with or without music, and the right to license others to include any or all of said compositions in song folios or lyric magazines with or without music.

(f) Any and all other rights of every and any nature now or hereafter existing under and by virtue of any common law rights and any copyrights and renewals and extensions thereof in any and all of such compositions. Writer grants to Publisher, without any compensation other than as specified herein, the perpetual right to use and publish and to permit others to use and publish Writer's name (including any professional name heretofore or hereafter adopted by Writer), likeness and biographical material, or any reproduction or simulation thereof and title of all compositions hereunder in connection with the printing, sale, advertising, distribution and exploitation of music, folios, recordings, performances, player rolls and otherwise concerning any of the compositions hereunder, and for any other purpose related to the business of Publisher, its affiliated and related companies, or to refrain therefrom. This right shall be exclusive during the term hereof and nonexclusive thereafter. Writer shall not authorize or permit the use of his name or likeness or biographical material concerning him, or other identification, or any reproduction

Exclusive Songwriter Agreement
Contracts Companion for Writers, by Tonya M. Evans-Walls
www.LiteraryLawGuide.com

or simulation thereof, for or in connection with any musical composition covered by this Agreement, other than by or for Publisher. Writer grants Publisher the right to refer to Writer as Publisher's "Exclusive Songwriter and Composer" or other similar appropriate appellation.

4. <u>Exclusivity</u>. From the date hereof and during the term of this Agreement, Writer will not write or compose or furnish or dispose of, any musical compositions, titles, lyrics or music, or any rights or interests therein whatsoever, nor participate in any manner with regard to the same for any person, firm or corporation other than Publisher, nor permit the use of his name or likeness as the writer or co-writer of any musical composition by any person, firm or corporation other than Publisher.

5. <u>Warranties, Representations, Covenants and Agreements</u>.

(a)   Writer hereby warrants, represents, covenants and agrees as follows: Writer has the full right, power and authority to enter into and perform this Agreement and to grant to and vest in Publisher all the rights herein set forth, free and clear of any and all claims, rights and obligations whatsoever; all the results and proceeds of the services of Writer hereunder, including all of the titles, lyrics, music and musical compositions, and each and every part thereof, delivered and to be delivered by Writer hereunder are and shall be new and original and capable of copyright protection throughout the entire world, and that no musical composition hereunder or any part hereof shall be an imitation or copy of, or shall infringe upon, any other material, or shall violate or infringe upon any common law or statutory rights of any party including, without limitation, contractual rights, copyrights and rights of privacy, and that Writer has not sold, assigned, leased, licensed or in any other way disposed of or encumbered the rights herein granted to Publisher, nor shall Writer sell, assign, lease, license or in any other way dispose of or encumber said rights.

(b)   Publisher represents and warrants that it is a company duly organized, validly existing, and in good standing under the laws of its jurisdiction of charter, having the full right, power and authority to enter into and perform this Agreement, and that it will use its best efforts to fully and faithfully fulfill its obligations hereon.

6. <u>Power of Attorney</u>. Writer does hereby irrevocably constitute, authorize, empower and appoint Publisher, or any of its officers, Writer's true and lawful attorney (with full power of substitution and delegation) in Writer's name, and in Writer's place and stead, or in Publisher's name, to take and do such action, and to make, sign, execute, acknowledge and deliver any and all instruments or documents which Publisher, from time to time, may deem desirable or necessary to vest in Publisher, its successors, assigns and licensees, any of the rights or interests granted by Writer hereunder, including but not limited to such documents required to secure to Publisher the renewals and extensions of copyrights throughout the world of musical compositions written or composed by Writer and owned by Publisher, and also such documents necessary to assign to Publisher, its successors and assigns, such renewal copyrights, and all rights therein for the terms of such renewals and extensions for the use and benefit of Publisher, its successors and assigns.

7. <u>Compensation</u>. Provided that Writer shall faithfully and completely perform the terms, covenants and conditions of this Agreement, Publisher hereby agrees to pay Writer for the services to be rendered by Writer under this Agreement and for the rights acquired and to be

Exclusive Songwriter Agreement
Contracts Companion for Writers, by Tonya M. Evans-Walls
www.LiteraryLawGuide.com

acquired hereunder, the following compensation based on the musical compositions which are the subject hereof.

(a) $.07 per copy for each piano copy and dance orchestration printed, published and sold in the United States and Canada by Publisher or its licensees, for which payment has been received by Publisher, after deduction or returns.

(b) ___ of the wholesale selling price upon each printed copy of each other arrangement and edition printed, published and sold in the United States and Canada by Publisher, for which payment has been received by Publisher, after deduction of returns, except that in the event that any composition shall be used or caused to be used, in whole or in part, in conjunction with one or more other musical compositions in a folio, album or other publication, Writer shall be entitled to receive that proportion of said ___ percent (___%) which the subject composition shall bear to the total number of musical compositions contained in such folio, album or other publication.

(c) Fifty percent (50%) of any and all net sums actually received (less any costs for collection) by Publisher in the United States from the exploitation in the United States and Canada by licensees of Publisher of mechanical rights, electrical transcription and reproducing rights, motion picture and television synchronization rights, printing rights (except as provided in (a) above), and all other rights (excepting public performing rights) therein, whether or not such licensees are affiliated with, owned in whole or in part by, or controlled by Publisher.

(d) Writer shall receive his public performance royalties throughout the world directly from his own affiliated performing rights society and shall have no claim whatsoever against Publisher for any royalties received by Publisher from any performing rights society which makes payment directly (or indirectly other than through Publisher) to writers, authors and composers.

(e) ___ of any and all net sums, after deduction of foreign taxes, actually received (less any costs for collection) by Publisher in the United States from sales, licenses and other uses of the subject musical compositions in countries outside of the United States and Canada (other than public performance royalties as hereinabove mentioned in (d) above) from collection agents, licensees, subpublishers or others, whether or not same are affiliated with, owned in whole or in part by, or controlled by Publisher.

(f) Publisher shall not be required to pay any royalties on professional or complimentary copies or any copies or mechanical derivative which are distributed gratuitously to performing artists, orchestra leaders and disc jockeys or for advertising, promotional or exploitation purposes. Furthermore, no royalties shall be payable to Writer on consigned copies unless paid for, and not until such time as an accounting therefor can properly be made.

(g) Royalties as hereinabove specified shall be payable to Writer in instances where Writer is the sole author of the entire composition, including the words and music thereof. However, in the event that one or more other songwriters are authors together with Writer on any composition (including songwriters employed by Publisher to add, change or translate the words or to revise or change the music), then the foregoing royalties shall be divided equally between Writer and the other songwriters of such composition unless another division of royalties is

Exclusive Songwriter Agreement
Contracts Companion for Writers, by Tonya M. Evans-Walls
www.LiteraryLawGuide.com

agreed upon in writing between the parties concerned.

(h) Except as herein expressly provided, no other royalties or moneys shall be paid to Writer.

(i) Writer agrees and acknowledges that Publisher shall have the right to withhold from the royalties payable to Writer hereunder such amount if any, as may be required under the applicable provisions of federal, state and local lax laws, and Writer agrees to execute such forms and other documents as may be required in connection therewith.

(j) In no event shall Writer be entitled to share in any advance payments, guarantee payments or minimum royalty payments which Publisher shall receive in connection with any subpublishing agreement, collection agreement, licensing agreement or other agreement covering the subject musical compositions.

8. <u>Other Agreements</u>. It is the intent of the parties hereto that the Term of this Agreement be coterminous and coextensive with the term of any recording contract entered into simultaneously herewith or during the Term hereof. Therefore the term of any such recording contract shall supersede the Term of this Agreement.

9. <u>Accounting</u>. Publisher will compute the total combined royalties earned by Writer pursuant to this Agreement and pursuant to any other agreement between Writer and Publisher, whether now in existence or entered into at any time subsequent hereto, on or before March 31 for the semiannual period ending the preceding December 31st and on or before September 30 for the semiannual period ending the preceding June 30th, and will submit to Writer the royalty statement for each such period together with the net amount of such royalties, if any, which shall be payable after deducting any and all unrecouped advances and chargeable costs under this Agreement or any other agreement between Writer and Publisher. Upon the submission of each statement, Publisher shall have the right to retain, as a reserve against subsequent charges, credits or returns, such portion of payable royalties as shall be necessary and appropriate in its best business judgment. All royalty statements rendered by Publisher to Writer shall be binding upon Writer and not subject to any objection by Writer for any reason unless specific written objection, stating the basis thereof, is submitted by Writer to Publisher within one (1) year from the date rendered. Writer or Writer's certified public accountant or legal representative on his behalf may, at Writer's expense, at reasonable intervals, examine Publisher's books insofar as same concern Writer, during Publisher's usual business hours and upon reasonable notice, for the purpose of verifying the accuracy of any royalty statement rendered to writer hereunder. Publisher's books relating to activities during any accounting period may only be examined as aforesaid during the one (1) year period following service by the Publisher of the royalty statement for said accounting period.

10. <u>Collaboration with other Writers</u>. Whenever Writer shall collaborate with any other person in the creation of any musical composition, any such musical composition shall be subject to the terms and conditions of this Agreement and Writer warrants and represents that prior to the collaboration with any other person, such other person shall be advised of this exclusive agreement and that all such compositions must be published by Publisher. In the event of such collaboration with any other person, Writer shall notify Publisher of the extent of interest that such other person may have in any such musical composition and Writer shall cause such other

Exclusive Songwriter Agreement
Contracts Companion for Writers, by Tonya M. Evans-Walls
www.LiteraryLawGuide.com

person to execute a separate songwriter's agreement with respect thereto, which agreement shall set forth the division of the songwriter's share of income between Writer and such other person, and Publisher shall make payment accordingly. If Publisher so desires, Publisher may request Writer to execute a separate agreement in Publisher's customary form with respect to each musical composition hereunder. Upon such request, Writer will promptly execute such agreement. Publisher shall have the right, pursuant to the terms and conditions hereof, to execute such agreement in behalf of Writer hereunder. Such agreement shall supplement and not supersede this Agreement. In the event of any conflict between the provisions of such agreement and this Agreement, the provisions of this Agreement shall govern. The failure of either of the parties hereto to execute such agreement, whether requested by Publisher or not, shall not affect the rights of each of the parties hereunder, including but not limited to the rights of Publisher to all of the musical compositions written and composed by Writer.

11.   <u>Writer's Services</u>. Writer agrees to perform the services required hereunder conscientiously and solely and exclusively for and as requested by Publisher. Writer is deemed to be a "writer for hire" hereunder with full rights of copyright and any renewals vested in Publisher. Writer further agrees to promptly and faithfully comply with all requirements and requests made by Publisher in connection with its business as set forth herein. Writer will deliver a manuscript copy of each musical composition hereunder immediately upon the completion or acquisition of such musical composition. Nothing contained in this Agreement shall obligate Publisher to exploit in any manner any of the rights granted to Publisher hereunder. Publisher, in its sole discretion, shall make studio facilities reasonably available for writer so that Writer, subject to the supervision and control of Publisher, may make demonstration records of the musical compositions hereunder and also for Writer to perform at such recording sessions. Writer shall not incur any liability for which Publisher may be responsible in connection with any demonstration record session without having first obtained Publisher's written approval as to the nature, extent and limit of such liability. In no event shall Writer incur any expense whatsoever in behalf of Publisher without first having received written authorization from Publisher. Writer shall not be entitled to any compensation (in addition to such compensation as may be otherwise provided for herein) with respect to services rendered in connection with such demonstration record recording sessions. Publisher shall advance the costs for the production of demonstration records, and one-half (1/2) of such costs shall be deemed additional recoupable nonreturnable advances to Writer and shall be deducted from royalties payable to Writer by Publisher under this Agreement or any other agreement between the parties. [**NOTE: Writers beware of "cross-collateralization clauses like this that allow publisher to recoup monies paid under one contract from proceeds earned on a different contract.**]. All recordings and reproductions made at demonstration recording session hereunder shall become the sole and exclusive property of Publisher, free of any claims whatsoever by Writer or any person deriving any rights from Writer.

Writer shall, from time to time, at Publisher's reasonable request, whenever the same will not unreasonably interfere with other professional engagements of Writer, appear for photography, artwork and other similar reasons under the direction of Publisher or its duly authorized agent, appear for interviews and other promotional purposes, and confer and consult with Publisher regarding Writer's services hereunder. Writer shall not be entitled to any compensation (other than applicable union scale if appropriate) for rendering such services, but shall be entitled to reasonable transportation and living expenses if such expenses must be incurred in order to render such services.

Exclusive Songwriter Agreement
Contracts Companion for Writers, by Tonya M. Evans-Walls
www.LiteraryLawGuide.com

12. Unique Services. Writer acknowledges that the services rendered hereunder are of a special, unique, unusual, extraordinary and intellectual character which gives them a peculiar value, the loss of which cannot be reasonably or adequately compensated in damages in an action at law, and that a breach by Writer of any of the provisions of this Agreement will cause Publisher great and irreparable injury and damage. Writer expressly agrees that Publisher shall be entitled to the remedies of injunction and other equitable relief to prevent a breach of this Agreement or any provision hereof, which relief shall be in addition to any other remedies, for damages or otherwise, which may be available to Publisher.

13. Actions. Publisher may take such action as it deems necessary, either in Writer's name or in its own name, against any person to protect all rights and interests acquired by Publisher hereunder. Writer will at Publisher's request, cooperate fully with Publisher in any controversy which may arise or litigation which may be brought concerning Publisher's rights and interests obtained hereunder. Publisher shall have the right, in its absolute discretion, to employ attorneys and to institute or defend any action or proceeding and to take any other proper steps to protect the right, title and interest of Publisher in and to each musical composition hereunder and every portion thereof and in that connection, to settle, compromise or in any other manner dispose of any matter, claim, action or proceeding and to satisfy any judgment that may be rendered, in any manner as Publisher in its sole discretion may determine. Any legal action brought by Publisher against an alleged infringer of any musical composition hereunder shall be initiated and prosecuted by Publisher, and if there is any recovery made by Publisher as a result thereof, after deduction of the expense of litigation, including but not limited to attorneys' fees and court costs, a sum equal to fifty percent (50%) of such net proceeds shall be paid to Writer. Writer agrees to and does hereby indemnify, save and hold Publisher harmless from any and all loss and damages (including reasonable attorneys' fees) arising out of or connected with any claim by a third party which is inconsistent with any of the warranties, representations, covenants or agreements made by Writer in this Agreement, and Writer agrees to reimburse Publisher, on demand, for any payment made by Publisher at any time after the date hereof with respect to any liability or claim to which the foregoing indemnity applies. Pending the determination of any such claim, Publisher may withhold payment of Royalties or other monies hereunder.

14. Notices. Any written notices which Publisher shall desire to give to Writer hereunder and all statements, royalties and other payments which shall be due to Writer hereunder shall be addressed to Writer at the address set forth on page 1 hereof until Writer shall give Publisher written notice of a new address. All notices which Writer shall desire to give to Publisher hereunder shall be addressed to Publisher at the address set forth on page 1 hereof until Publisher shall give Writer written notice of a new address. All notices shall be delivered by hand (to any member of Writer if Writer shall be the addresses or to an officer of Publisher if Publisher shall be the addressee) or served by mail, postage prepaid, or telegraph, charges prepaid, addressed as aforesaid. The date of making personal service or of mailing or of depositing in a telegraph office, whichever shall be first, shall be deemed the date of service.

15. Entire Agreement. This agreement supersedes any and all prior negotiations, understandings, and agreements between the parties hereto with respect to the subject matter hereof. Each of the parties acknowledges and agrees that neither party has made any representations or promises in connection with this Agreement or the subject matter hereof not contained herein.

Exclusive Songwriter Agreement
Contracts Companion for Writers, by Tonya M. Evans-Walls
www.LiteraryLawGuide.com

16. <u>Modification, Waiver, Illegality</u>. This agreement may not be canceled, altered, modified, amended or waived, in whole or in part, in any way, except by an instrument in writing signed by both Publisher and Writer. The waiver by Publisher of any breach of this Agreement in any one or more instances, shall in no way be construed as a waiver of any subsequent breach (whether or not of a similar nature) of this Agreement by Writer. If any part of this Agreement shall be held to be void, invalid or unenforceable, it shall not affect the validity of the balance of this Agreement. The agreement shall be governed by and construed under the laws and judicial decisions of the Commonwealth of Pennsylvania.

17. <u>Termination</u>. Publisher shall have the right to terminate this Agreement upon thirty (30) days prior written notice.

18. <u>Assignment</u>. Publisher shall have the right to assign this Agreement or any of its rights hereunder to any party. This agreement shall inure to the benefit of and be binding upon each of the parties hereto and their respective successors, assigns, heirs, executors, administrators and legal and personal representatives.

19. <u>Attorneys' Fees</u>. In the event of any action suit or proceeding by Publisher against Writer under this Agreement, in which Publisher shall prevail, Publisher shall be entitled to recover reasonable attorneys' fees and costs of said action, suit or proceeding.

20. <u>Division of Royalties</u>. As has hereinabove been provided, the word "Writer" as used throughout this Agreement, refers collectively to all of the undersigned, all of whom are members of the group known as _____, provided however, that all restrictive and exclusive provisions herein contained apply individually to each of the undersigned. Notwithstanding any provision to the contrary contained in this Agreement, it is understood and acknowledged that Writer's royalties for any musical composition hereunder shall be payable only to the undersigned individual or individuals whose name or names are submitted in writing to Publisher as the actual composer or composers of said composition and shall not be payable to any others of the undersigned unless Publisher is advised in writing to the contrary at the time such composition is submitted to Publisher hereunder. In the event this Agreement is terminated for any reason whatsoever as to any of the undersigned who comprise Writer, this Agreement shall nevertheless remain in full force and effect as to each of the undersigned comprising Writer with whom this Agreement is not so terminated.

IN WITNESS WHEREOF the parties hereto have executed this Agreement as of the day and year first above written.

By:

_____   TIN:_____

_____   TIN:_____

_____   TIN:_____

Co-Publishing Agreement
Contracts Companion for Writers, by Tonya M. Evans-Walls
www.LiteraryLawGuide.com

Patsi Pen
123 Fountain Lane
Philadelphia, PA 19199

DATE

Dear Ms. Pen,

The following, when signed by you and by us, will constitute the terms and conditions of the exclusive co-publishing agreement between you and us.

1. <u>Scope of Agreement</u>:

(a)   Subject to those subparagraph (b), below, you and we will each own an undivided fifty percent (50%) share of the copyright in the songs (and all derivative works based thereon) listed on the attached Schedule "A" (referred to below as the "Subject Compositions"). We shall have exclusive right to administer the Subject Compositions throughout the world for the full term of copyright, and any renewals and extensions thereof.

(b)   Although it is intended that we and our foreign subsidiaries, affiliates and licensees have the fullest possible rights to administer and exploit the Subject Compositions, to utilize your name and likeness in connection therewith and to execute PA forms (and other routine copyright documents) in your name and on your behalf as your attorney-in-fact (which appointment is coupled with an interest and is therefore irrevocable), neither we nor they shall do any of the following without your prior written consent in each instance (which consent shall not be unreasonably withheld by you):

(i)   Authorize any change in the English-language title and/or lyric of any Subject Composition, alter the harmonic structure of any Subject Composition, or alter the melody of any Subject Composition (except insubstantial changes necessary to accommodate the syllabic requirements of foreign languages);

(ii)   Issue a mechanical license for the use of any Subject Composition at less than the then prevailing statutory or society rate, except in connection with those types of uses for which reduced-rate licenses are customarily granted in the country in question;

(iii)   Authorize the use of the title of any Subject Composition as the title of a play, film or TV program, or authorize the dramatization of any Subject Composition;

(iv)   Authorize the synchronization of any Subject Composition in (A) a film or TV program bearing a rating of "X" or the equivalent, (B) any political advertisement, or (C) in any advertisement promoting morally objectionable products or services;

(v)   Authorize the use of any Subject Composition in a way that would materially and negatively impact the long term value of a Subject Composition.

Co-Publishing Agreement
Contracts Companion for Writers, by Tonya M. Evans-Walls
www.LiteraryLawGuide.com

2. <u>Collection and Division of Income</u>:

   (a)   Subject to any rights and/or remedies which may be available to us in the event of a material breach of this agreement on your part not cured as provided in par. 5(c), below, we will be entitled to collect (and shall employ our best efforts) all writer/publisher income (except the writer's share of public performances collected by societies and any other amount normally paid directly to songwriters by a disbursing agent) generated by the Subject Compositions (including pre-Term earnings).

      (i)   (A) Net Income from Subject Compositions shall be divided 50% to us, 50% to you.

             (B) As used herein, "Net Income" shall mean all amounts received by us, or credited to our account in reduction of an advance, from licensees and performing and mechanical rights societies ("Gross Receipts") after deduction of writer royalties as per the annexed Schedule "B" and (1) actual and reasonable out-of-pocket collection costs (including local subpublisher fees or income shares) (2) out-of-pocket copyright registration costs, (3) costs of lead sheets, and (4) demo costs (approved by both parties in writing) to the extent not recouped from writer royalties.

      (ii)   For the purposes of this paragraph, Gross Receipts on printed materials sold (and paid for) shall be deemed to be:

      (iii)   (A) Outside of the U.S. and Canada ___% of the marked or suggested retail list price (or the price deemed to be the local equivalent, in any country in which there are no marked or suggested retail list prices) ("list") (prorated in the case of mixed folios and other editions not consisting entirely of Subject Compositions);

             (B) In the U.S. and Canada, ___% of list on piano/vocal sheet music, ___% of list on folios other than "fake books" or "educational editions", ___% of list on "fake books" and "educational editions" (prorated in either event in the case of mixed folios and other mixed editions), on copies sold and paid for;

             (C) In the case of amounts received from third-party print licensees your co-publisher's share shall be 25% while the writer's share shall be 50%; and

             (D) Print royalties are subject to proration where only part of the composition is a Subject Composition.

      (iv)   Gross Receipts received from our affiliates and licensees outside of the U.S. and Canada shall be deemed to be 80% of mechanical income from original records, 60% of mechanical income from Cover Records, 60% of the publisher's share of public performance income, and 80% of other categories of income (other than print).

3. <u>Accounting and Payment</u>:

   (a)   We will account to you (and make payment where appropriate) within 60 days following the end of each semi-annual calendar period, being June 30 and December 31. However, if the amount due for a specific statement is less than Fifty Dollars ($50), payment may be deferred until the aggregate amount due to you exceeds Fifty Dollars ($50).

Co-Publishing Agreement
Contracts Companion for Writers, by Tonya M. Evans-Walls
www.LiteraryLawGuide.com

(b)   We will only be required to account and pay with respect to amounts actually received by us in the U.S. (or credited to our account in reduction of a previous advance received by us in the U.S.).

(i)   You (or a certified public accountant or legal representative on your behalf) shall have the right to audit our books and records as to each statement for a period of 2 years after such statement is received (or deemed received as provided below). Legal action with respect to a specific accounting statement or the accounting period to which such statement relates shall be barred if not commenced in a court of competent jurisdiction within 3 years after such statement is received (or deemed received as provided below).

(ii)   For the purposes of calculating such time periods, you shall be deemed to have received a statement when due unless we receive notice of nonreceipt from you (in the manner prescribed in paragraph 6, below) within 30 days thereafter. However, your failure to give such notice shall not affect your right to receive such statement (and, if applicable, your royalty and/or net income payment) after such thirty-day period.

(c)   In "blocked currency" situations, we shall not be required to pay you until the blockage shall have been removed, but if requested to do so, we shall deposit blocked currency royalties in the local currency in a depository of your choice. The exchange rates used by third parties in accounting to us shall be used by us in accountings hereunder.

(d)   All payments hereunder shall be subject to all applicable taxation statutes, regulations and treaties.

4.   <u>Warranties and Representations</u>:

(a)   By your signature below, you warrant and represent (1) that you have the right to grant the rights granted to us hereunder, (2) that the Subject Compositions do not infringe any third party's rights or violate any applicable criminal statute, including but not limited to such third party's copyright, trademark, service mark, or right of privacy or publicity, (3) that the Subject Compositions are not defamatory and (4) that your music publishing designee will affiliate with ASCAP, BMI or another recognized performing rights society to which the writers of the Subject Compositions are affiliated, and you will immediately advise us of said affiliation.

(b)   Except as set forth in the annexed Schedule "C" (if applicable), neither you nor your music publishing designee, nor anyone acting on your and/or your music publishing designee's behalf or deriving rights from or through you or your music publishing designee (A) has received or will receive an advance, loan or other payment from a performing rights society, record company or other third party which is or may be recoupable from (or otherwise subject to offset against) moneys which would otherwise be collectible by us hereunder, (B) is presently subject to any so-called "controlled compositions" clause under a recording agreement or (C) is presently subject to any provision of a recording agreement which would allow a record company to charge any amount against mechanical royalties.

(c)   Notwithstanding the foregoing, in the event that any record company to whom you (or an entity furnishing your services) are or may hereafter be under contract charges any advance(s) or other amount(s) against mechanical royalties earned by the Subject Compositions from recordings made under such recording agreement or reduces the amount of mechanical royalties otherwise due to you because the mechanical royalties payable with respect to "outside

Co-Publishing Agreement
Contracts Companion for Writers, by Tonya M. Evans-Walls
www.LiteraryLawGuide.com

material" embodied in your recordings causes aggregate mechanical royalties to exceed the per-record maximum rate(s) prescribed in the controlled compositions clause of your recording agreement, then, in addition to any other rights and remedies available to us, we shall be entitled to (A) send a letter of direction (a form of which is annexed hereto as "Exhibit 1") in your name advising your record company of the terms of this paragraph 4 and instructing such record company (upon recoupment from record and/or video royalties of any portion(s) of the advance(s) or other amount(s) so charged) to re-credit us directly to the same extent (not to exceed the total amount originally recouped from or charged against mechanical royalties) and (B) reimburse ourselves from any and all moneys (including your writer/publisher royalties) earned hereunder, for any amount charged against mechanical royalties, except to the extent later recovered through the re-crediting process.

(d)   In the event of a breach of this paragraph 4, we shall (in addition to any other remedies available to us) be entitled to reimburse ourselves from moneys otherwise becoming due to you or your music publishing designee hereunder to the extent that moneys are not collectible by us by reason thereof.

5. Indemnities; Cure of Breaches:

(a)   Each party will indemnify the other against any loss or damage (including court costs and reasonable attorneys' fees) due to a breach of this agreement by that party which results in a judgment against the other party or which is settled with the other party's prior written consent (not to be unreasonably withheld). In addition, your indemnity shall extend to the "deductible" under our errors-and-omissions policy without regard to judgment or settlement. Each party is entitled to be notified of any action against the other brought with respect to any Subject Composition, and to participate in the defense thereof by counsel of its choice, at its sole cost and expense. In the event that one of us refuses to approve a settlement which the other party considers reasonable, the party refusing its consent shall assume the further defense of the subject claim, action or proceeding.

(b)   If a claim is made against us, we may withhold a reasonable amount from moneys due or to become due to you, but we will refund it (together with interest on the amount released at the regular savings and loan passbook interest rate prevailing in [insert city] from time to time during the period of withholding) if (and to the extent that) suit is not brought with respect to that sum within 1 year thereafter, and we won't withhold moneys hereunder if (and to the extent that) you provide us with a satisfactory commercial surety bond.

(c)   Neither party will be deemed in breach unless the other party gives notice and the notified party fails to cure within 30 days after receiving notice; provided, that if the alleged breach is of such a nature that it cannot be completely cured within 30 days, the notified party will not be deemed to be in breach if the notified party commences the curing of the alleged breach within such thirty-day period and proceeds to complete the curing thereof with due diligence within a reasonable time thereafter. However, either party shall have the right to seek injunctive relief to prevent a threatened breach of this agreement by the other party. All payments required to be made by us hereunder shall be subject to any rights and/or remedies which may otherwise be available to us in the event of a breach of this agreement on your part not cured in the manner prescribed above, and to any withholding which may be required by the rules and regulations of any taxing jurisdiction having authority.

6. Notices: Notices shall be sent by traceable mail to you and us at the above addresses or any other addresses the parties designate by notice in like manner. Statements (and payments, if applicable) shall be sent by ordinary mail. If the party's consent is required, it shall not be

Co-Publishing Agreement
Contracts Companion for Writers, by Tonya M. Evans-Walls
www.LiteraryLawGuide.com

unreasonably withheld (unless expressly provided otherwise herein) and shall be deemed given unless the notified party gives notice of nonconsent within 15 days after receipt of notice requesting consent.

7. <u>Law and Forum</u>: This agreement has been entered into in, and is to be interpreted in accordance with the laws of, the Commonwealth of Pennsylvania. All actions or proceedings seeking the interpretation and/or enforcement of this Agreement shall be brought only in the State or Federal Courts located in Los Angeles County, all parties hereby submitting themselves to the jurisdiction of such courts for such purpose.

[ATL: Also consider using arbitration instead of litigation or for lesser controversies.]

Very truly yours,

LOVELY PUBLISHING LLC

By: _____

AGREED AND ACCEPTED:

By: _____
     Patsi Pen

TIN: _____

Co-Publishing Agreement
Contracts Companion for Writers, by Tonya M. Evans-Walls
www.LiteraryLawGuide.com

SCHEDULE "A"

Titles	Composers/%	% Controlled

Co-Publishing Agreement
Contracts Companion for Writers, by Tonya M. Evans-Walls
www.LiteraryLawGuide.com

SCHEDULE "B"

WRITER ROYALTIES

(1)   <u>U.S. and Canada</u>:

   <u>Print</u>: (all on net paid sales):

   Piano/vocal sheet: 7 cents

      Folios (other than "fake books" or "educational editions"): 12 1/2% of wholesale (prorated in the case of "mixed" folios to reflect number of royalty-bearing compositions);

      "Fake books" and "educational editions": 10% of wholesale (subject to same pro-ration);

(2)   <u>Mechanical Royalties</u>: 50% of gross receipts

(3)   <u>Performance Royalties</u>: if collected directly by us and not through a society: 50% of gross receipts

(4)   <u>Foreign Income</u>: 50% of gross receipts

(5)   <u>Other Income</u>: 50% of gross receipts; provided, that Writer shall not be entitled to receive any portion of any amount received by us from a source which pays writer an equivalent amount directly (including but not limited to distributions from a performing rights society and direct payments of portions of any blank tape tax or charge which may be enacted by Congress if writers and publishers are paid separately).

(6)   <u>Demo Costs</u>: To the extent approved by both parties in writing in advance, we shall pay for the cost of making demonstration records of the Subject Compositions. One-half (1/2) of a pro rata share corresponding to Writer's percentage of the Subject Compositions of such total costs shall be deemed additional advances to Writer hereunder.

   Above royalties to be prorated where only part of the subject composition is subject to this agreement.

Co-Publishing Agreement
Contracts Companion for Writers, by Tonya M. Evans-Walls
www.LiteraryLawGuide.com

<u>SCHEDULE "C"</u>

(Pursuant to subparagraph 4(b), if applicable.)

Co-Publishing Agreement
Contracts Companion for Writers, by Tonya M. Evans-Walls
www.LiteraryLawGuide.com

EXHIBIT 1

DATE

[Performing Rights Org.]

To Whom It May Concern:

You are hereby authorized and directed to pay to my administrator, Lovely Publishing, LLC ("Administrator"), at _____, and I hereby assign to Administrator, all moneys payable from and after the date hereof (regardless of when earned) as my share of the publisher's public performance royalties with respect to the compositions described below:

COMPOSITION   COMPOSERS

Copies of all statements shall be sent to Administrator and to us.

The foregoing authorization and direction shall remain in full force and effect until modified or terminated by both the undersigned and Administrator.

Very truly yours,

Licensing Agreement
Contracts Companion for Writers,   by Tonya M. Evans-Walls
www.LiteraryLawGuide.com

LICENSING AGREEMENT

THIS LICENSING AGREEMENT (the "Agreement") is entered into as of the ___ day of _____, 200_, (the "Effective Date") between XYZ PRODUCTIONS, LLC, a Pennsylvania limited liability company, with its principal place of business at PO Box 12345, Philadelphia PA, (hereinafter referred to as the "Licensee") and PATSI PEN, an individual, located at 1234 Mockingbird Lane, Philadelphia, PA (hereinafter referred to as the "Licensor") with respect to the licensing of certain rights in the Licensor's creative work(s) (hereinafter referred to as the "Property").

TERMS

1.   Description of Property. The Licensee wishes to license certain rights in the Property that the Licensor has created and/or owns and which is described as follows:

[Insert description]

2.   Delivery Date. The Licensor agrees to deliver the Property on or before _____, subject to Paragraph 3.

3.   Grant of License. Upon receipt of full payment pursuant to Paragraphs 7 and 8 below, Licensor grants to the Licensee the following [irrevocable] [exclusive/nonexclusive] rights in the Property:

[Insert description of rights licensed]

4.   Term. The term of this Agreement will begin on the Effective Date and will continue for the full term of Licensor's copyright in the Property, including any renewals and extensions thereof.

5.   Territory. Worldwide in all media now known or hereinafter invented.

6.   Reservation of Rights. All rights not expressly granted hereunder are reserved to the Licensor.

Licensing Agreement
Contracts Companion for Writers,   by Tonya M. Evans-Walls
www.LiteraryLawGuide.com

7.   <u>License Fee</u>. Licensee agrees to pay the following one-time flat fee for the license granted herein: _____.

8.   <u>Payment Terms</u>. Licensee agrees to pay the Licensor in US currency within five (5) business days of execution by both parties of this Agreement.

9.   <u>Other Uses of Property</u>. If Licensee wishes to make any additional uses of the Property, Licensee shall request permission from the Licensor and make any such payments as are agreed to between the parties at that time.

10.   <u>Alteration of Property</u>. Other than as permitted in Paragraph 3, Licensee shall not make or permit any alterations, whether by adding or removing material from the Property, without the permission of the Licensor.

11.   <u>Copyright Notice</u>. Copyright notice in the name of the Licensor shall, to the extent commercially and artistically practicable, in Licensee's discretion, accompany the Property.

12.   <u>Credit</u>. Credit in the name of the Licensor shall accompany the Property, and any related advertising and promotional materials, if and when they are created and distributed. Notwithstanding the foregoing, any inadvertent failure by Licensee to do so shall not constitute a material breach of this Agreement. Licensee will use its best efforts to remedy or cause to be remedied such inadvertent failure to the extent reasonably possible and within a reasonable time after being notified by Licensor.

13.   <u>Representation, Warranty and Indemnifications</u>.

    A.   Licensor represents and warrants that she has the exclusive right to grant permission to Licensee to use the Property.

    B.   Licensor and Licensee each indemnify and hold the other harmless from and against any and all claims, actions, liability, damages, costs, and expenses, including reasonable legal fees and expenses, incurred by the other as a result of the breach of her respective warranties, representations, and/or undertakings pursuant to this Agreement.

14.   <u>Confidentiality</u>.

    A.   Confidential Information is defined as information about the disclosing

Licensing Agreement
Contracts Companion for Writers, by Tonya M. Evans-Walls
www.LiteraryLawGuide.com

party's business that is proprietary and confidential, which shall include all business, financial, technical and other information of a party marked or designated by such party as "confidential" or "proprietary," or information which, by the nature of the circumstances surrounding the disclosure, ought in good faith to be treated as confidential.

B.   Each party will:

(i) not disclose to any third party or use any Confidential Information disclosed to it by the other except as expressly permitted in this Agreement; and

(ii) take all reasonable measures to maintain the confidentiality of all Confidential Information of the other party in its possession or, which will in no event be less than the measures it uses to maintain the confidentiality of its own information of similar importance.

C.   Notwithstanding the foregoing, each party may disclose Confidential Information as follows:

(i) to the extent required by a court of competent jurisdiction or other governmental authority or otherwise as required by law; or

(ii) on a "need-to-know" basis under an obligation of confidentiality to its legal counsel, accountants, banks and other sources and their advisors.

D.   The terms and conditions of this Agreement will be deemed to be the Confidential Information of each party and will not be disclosed without the written consent of the other party.

Licensing Agreement
Contracts Companion for Writers, by Tonya M. Evans-Walls
www.LiteraryLawGuide.com

15.   <u>Termination</u>.

A.   Either party may terminate this Agreement if the other party materially breaches its obligations either to deliver the Property or to render payment hereunder and such breach remains uncured for thirty (30) days following the notice to the breaching party of the breach.

B.   The provisions of this Section 15 (Termination), Section 14 (Confidentiality), Section 13 (Representation, Warranty, and Indemnifications), and Section 16 (Arbitration) will survive any termination or expiration of this Agreement.

C.   Notwithstanding the foregoing, once delivery and payment have been completed, this License shall remain in full force for the duration of the Term stated hereinabove.

16.   <u>Arbitration</u>. All disputes arising under this Agreement shall be submitted to confidential binding arbitration in Philadelphia, Pennsylvania and shall be settled in accordance with the rules of the American Arbitration Association. Judgment upon the arbitration award may be entered in any court having jurisdiction thereof. The prevailing party shall receive reasonable attorney's fees.

17.   <u>Governing Law</u>. This Agreement shall be governed by the laws of the Commonwealth of Pennsylvania.

18.   <u>Assignment</u>. Neither party may assign this Agreement, in whole or in part, without the other party's written consent (which will not be unreasonably withheld), except that no such consent will be required in connection with a merger, reorganization or sale of all, or substantially all, of such party's assets, or assignment to a company owned or directed by the assignee. Any attempt to assign this Agreement other than as permitted above will be null and void.

19.   <u>Notice</u>. Any notice under this Agreement will be in writing and delivered to the other party by personal delivery, express courier, confirmed facsimile, confirmed email or certified or registered mail, return receipt requested. Notices will be sent to a party at its address set forth above and as follows:

<u>Licensor's Attorney/Representative</u>

[Contact Information]

Licensing Agreement
Contracts Companion for Writers,   by Tonya M. Evans-Walls
www.LiteraryLawGuide.com

Licensee's Attorney/Representative

[Contact Information]

20.   No Agency. The parties are independent contractors and will have no power or authority to assume or create any obligation or responsibility on behalf of each other. This Agreement will not be construed to create or imply any partnership, agency or joint venture.

21.   Severability. Should any provision of this Agreement be void or unenforceable for any reason, such provisions shall be deemed omitted or modified to the extent required by law and this Agreement with such provisions omitted or so modified shall remain in full force and effect.

22.   Entire Agreement. This Agreement shall be binding upon the parties hereto, their heirs, successors, assigns, and personal representatives. This Agreement constitutes the entire understanding between the parties. Its terms can be modified only by an instrument in writing signed by both parties. A waiver of a breach of any of the provisions of this Agreement shall not be construed as a continuing waiver of other breaches of the same or other provisions hereof.

IN WITNESS WHEREOF, the parties hereto have signed this Agreement as of the date first set forth above. This Agreement may be executed in counterparts.

ACCEPTED AND AGREED TO:

LICENSOR   XYZ PRODUCTIONS, LLC

_____   By: _____
PATSI PEN

SSN: _____

Permission Request Form
Contracts Companion for Writers, by Tonya M. Evans-Walls
www.LiteraryLawGuide.com

PERMISSION REQUEST FORM

The Undersigned hereby grants permission to _____, (hereinafter referred to as the "Author"), located at _____, and to the Author's successors and assigns, to use the material specified in this Permission Form (hereinafter referred to a "Material") in the book titled _____ (the "Work") to be published by _____.

1.   The Material.

     A.   Title and/or nature of Material: [Insert].

     B.   Exact description of Material: [Insert].

     C.   Source of the Material: [Insert].

2.   Publication Information.

     A.   The Material has [has not] been previously published.

     B.   [If published, include copyright notice and ownership information.]

3.   Grant of Rights. Author, or Author's designees, shall have the irrevocable right to use the Material in the Work and in any future revisions, editions, and electronic versions thereof, including nonexclusive world rights in all languages. It is understood that the grant of this permission shall in no way restrict republication of the Material by the Undersigned or others authorized by the Undersigned.

[Alternate Clause: Grant of Rights Author, or Author's designees, shall have the exclusive and irrevocable right to use the Material in the Work and in any future revisions, editions, and electronic versions thereof, including nonexclusive world rights in all languages.]

4.   Copyright Notice and Credit. On publication the Material shall be accompanied by a copyright notice as follows: _____ and a

Permission Request Form

Permission Request Form
Contracts Companion for Writers, by Tonya M. Evans-Walls
www.LiteraryLawGuide.com

credit line as follows: The _____ is reproduced from [inert name/description of material], by _____ © [date] by _____. Used with the permission of the [publisher/author], _____.

5.   Miscellaneous Provisions. [Insert other provisions, if any: _____.]

6.   Ownership.   The Undersigned warrants that he/she has the exclusive right to grant permission to use the Material.

[Alternate insert: The Undersigned does not have the exclusive right to permit use of the Material and permission must also be granted by the following owners: _____.]

AGREED TO AND ACCEPTED:

_____   _____
[Name]   Date

Business Name: _____

Business Address: _____

City, State Zip:_____

Business Telephone:_____   Fax:_____

E-mail:_____

Release Forms

Interviewee/Model Release Forms
Contracts Companion for Writers
www.LiteraryLawGuide.com

Interviewee Release Form

I, the undersigned, do hereby consent to be interviewed on [insert date(s)] and to be recorded during said interview by _____ (the "Interviewer"). I hereby grant and assign to Interviewer and her heirs, legal representatives, agents, affiliates and assigns, all right, title and interest in the physical [audio/video] recordings (the "Recordings") and any derivatives, adaptations and editions thereof and all transcripts of such recordings (the "Transcripts" and, together with the Recordings, the Materials). Notwithstanding the foregoing, I retain all copyright, performance and other rights I may otherwise have in the underlying information.

[NOTE: This can also be revised for conference participants and performer releases to cover readings, performances, lectures, concerts and panel discussions).]

Purpose of Use: I understand the underlying information embodied in the Materials may be used for the following private and/or public purposes: [describe use or uses – scholarly, educational, archival, promotional, commercial, internal/staff use]. The Materials may be reproduced, published, broadcast and re-broadcast (applicable), in print, audio, video, audiovisual, electronic, multimedia formats and or any other format now known or hereafter developed and the Materials may be used in whole or in part without restriction.

Exceptions: _____.

Use of Persona: I hereby consent to the Interviewer's use of my name, voice or other sound effects, image, likeness, and statements (collectively my "Persona") without my further approval.

Exceptions: _____.

Waiver of Royalties: I hereby waive my right to any royalties or future consideration for my participation in this interview or the rights and permissions granted herein.

[ALT: Include a statement about the type, amount, manner, method and timing of payments.]

Representations and Warranties: I hereby affirm that I am at least eighteen years of age (or the age of majority in this jurisdiction); I am of sound mind; I have the right to enter into this legally binding and enforceable agreement; my statements are accurate, factual and do not infringe on the copyright, privacy and publicity rights of any person or entity and do not defame any person or entity; I have reviewed this release prior to its execution; and I fully understand the contents thereof.

[NOTE: If interviewing a minor, you must get the consent of a parent or guardian.]

AGREED and ACCEPTED this ___ day of _____, 200_.

Signed:_____

Interviewee/Model Release Forms
Contracts Companion for Writers
www.LiteraryLawGuide.com

Address:_____

Phone:_____

Interviewee/Model Release Forms
Contracts Companion for Writers
www.LiteraryLawGuide.com

Model Release Form

I, _____, hereby irrevocably grant to _____ (the "Photographer") and his/her heirs, legal representatives, agents, affiliates and assigns the unrestricted right regarding my photographic image, likeness and persona (collectively referred to as "Persona") to copyright and use, re-use, publish, and republish photographic portraits or pictures (and copies thereof) of me or in which I may be included in whole, part, composite or distortion of character or form, including, without limitation, use of my legal name or a fictitious name, in any manner and form, made through the universe in any and all media now or hereafter developed for illustration, art, promotion, advertising, trade, or any other purpose whatsoever and any printed material in connection therewith.

Waiver of Approval: Further, I hereby relinquish any right to examine or approve the Photographer's use of my Persona in connection with any products, promotional copy or printed matter that may be created in connection therewith or the use to which it may be applied.

     Exceptions:_____.

Release: I hereby release, discharge and agree to hold harmless Photographer, his/her heirs, legal representatives, agents, affiliates or assigns, from any and all liability by virtue of any blurring, distortion, alteration, optical illusion, or use in composite form whether intentional or otherwise, that may occur or be produced in the taking of said picture or in any subsequent processing thereof, as well as any publication or broadcast thereof, including, without limitation, any claims for copyright infringement, libel, right of publicity or right of privacy.

     Exceptions:_____.

Representations and Warranties: I hereby affirm that I am at least eighteen years of age (or the age of majority in this jurisdiction); I am of sound mind; I have the right to enter into this legally binding and enforceable agreement; I have reviewed this release prior to its execution; I fully understand the contents thereof.

This agreement shall be binding upon me and my heirs, legal representatives, agents, affiliates and assigns.

AGREED and ACCEPTED this ___ day of _____, 200_.

Signed:_____

Address:_____

Interviewee/Model Release Forms
Contracts Companion for Writers
www.LiteraryLawGuide.com

Phone:_____

Witness:_____

Glossary

acceptance A publisher's approval of a delivered manuscript (or other item to be delivered).

ASCAP American Society of Composers, Authors and Publishers.

author Generally a writer, but in the context of the Copyright Act, it includes anyone who creates an original work.

assignment Transfer of copyright ownership from one person or entity to another.

BMI Broadcast Music, Incorporated.

bundle of rights All of the individual rights conferred by copyright: namely the right to copy, distribute, prepare derivative works, display publicly, and perform publicly.

collaboration agreement An agreement between two or more people who contribute work to a book or other creation.

collective works Defined in the Copyright Act as "a number of contributions, constituting separate and independent works in themselves . . . assembled into a collective whole." Individuals or entities who combine individual contributions into one collection hold the copyright in the collection as a whole. But the individual authors retain rights to the individual work apart from the collection. This limitation is found in section 201(c) of the Copyright Act: "In the absence of an express transfer of the copyright or of any rights under it, the owner of the copyright in the collective work is presumed to have acquired only the privilege of reproducing and distributing the contribution as part of that particular collective work, any revision of that collective work, and any later collective work in the same series." Thus, other than the rights to reproduce and distribute the collection, and the right to create a derivative work of the collection, the individual contributors to the collection retain the copyright to their individual contributions.

common law A body of law that is made up of cases rather than laws enacted by legislation.

consideration A legal concept best described as the benefit or detriment that induces someone to make a promise and enter into a contractual arrangement based on the terms, conditions, rights, and obligations agreed to by the parties involved.

copyright The exclusive rights of a copyright owner of a work to make and distribute copies, prepare derivative works, and perform and display the work publicly.

copyright registration Submitting the copyrighted work to the Copyright Office, pursuant to the rules and guidelines set forth by that office.

damages Generally, a sum of money paid in compensation for loss or injury.

delivery The act of giving the manuscript (or other item to be delivered) to the publisher.

delivery date The stipulated date by which an author must deliver the manuscript to the publisher.

detrimental reliance See promissory estoppel.

execute To complete, make valid, or give effect by signing.

first proceeds The money received by an author from any sale or license of any rights in his or her copyrighted work to a third party (someone other than the company that originally agreed to publish the work). This situation may arise if the publisher and author enter into a publishing contract, the publisher pays the author an advance, and later the publisher rejects the author's manuscript. If the author then sells the work to another publisher, the first publisher may require the author to repay it from the first money payable to the author as a result of the second publishing deal.

independent contractor One who is self-employed and has the right to control the means and methods of performing work.

joint work A work prepared by two or more authors with the intention that their contributions be merged into inseparable or interdependent parts of a unitary whole.

legalese Expressions used primarily by lawyers to articulate and discuss legal issues.

licensing agreement An agreement that sets forth the terms that allow others the limited right to use your work (or for you to use the work of others). You remain the owner of the copyright. A license can be exclusive (only the licensee can use it) or non-exclusive (the licensee can use your work but cannot exclude others from doing so).

literary works Works, other than audiovisual works, expressed in words, numbers, or other verbal or numerical symbols or indicia, regardless of the nature of the material objects, such as books, periodicals, manuscripts, phonorecords, film, tapes, disks, or cards, in which they are embodied.

phonorecords Material objects, such as cassette tapes, CDs, or LPs—but not motion picture soundtracks on which sounds are recorded and which combine moving images and sound.

prima facie A legal term of Latin origin that refers to a piece of evidence which is valid "on its face" or "on its first appearance" unless and until proved otherwise.

primary rights The main set of rights that a publisher intends to exploit. Generally, this means the right to publish the work in book form (hardcover and paperback rights, and perhaps book club rights and so forth). Compare with **subsidiary rights** below.

privacy, right of The right to be left alone. The three generally recognized invasions of privacy include intrusion, unreasonable publicity, and false light.

promissory estoppel If one party to a contract relies, to his or her disadvantage, on the promise of another, a court may enforce an agreement even if it is not considered a legally binding contract due to less than adequate consideration. Also referred to as detrimental reliance.

publication The distribution of copies or phonorecords (includes records, CDs, cassettes, and the like) of a work to the public by sale or other transfer of ownership, or by rental, lease, or lending. The offering to distribute copies or phonorecords to a group of persons for purposes of further distribution, public performance, or public display constitutes publication. A public performance or display of a work does not of itself constitute publication.

publicity, right of A person's exclusive right to use his or her name, likeness, or other aspect of his or her persona, and the right to prevent others from using those aspects without authorization.

publisher A person or entity that produces any periodical, magazine, newspaper, book, manual, advertising materials, or other similar material, whether in printed, electronic, or other form.

revision period The period of time a publisher grants to an author to revise a manuscript.

SESAC Society of European Songwriters, Artists and Composers.

subsidiary rights The secondary set of rights that may be transferred to a publisher. This may include rights that exist as a result of the primary rights, for example, audio, motion picture and TV, dramatic, mass market paperback, and electronic rights. Compare with **primary rights** above.

vetting A line-by-line review of a manuscript for potential legal issues.

work-made-for-hire A legal doctrine which says that for purposes of copyright protection, the one who commissioned the work to be created by an independent contractor, and not the creator of the work, is the owner of that work; and that an employer owns the copyright to any artistic or literary work that is created by an employee on company time using company equipment.

Index

About the Author

Tonya M. Evans-Walls is the managing attorney of a Philadelphia-based law firm that concentrates in the areas of entertainment law (literary, music and film), intellectual property (copyright and trademark), estate planning, and municipal finance. She is the chair of the Pennsylvania Bar Association's Sports, Entertainment, and Art Law Committee; visiting professor of law (property and intellectual property) at Widener University School of Law; and former adjunct professor of music licensing, publishing, and copyright at York College of Pennsylvania. She is also a nationally recognized speaker who presents to various audiences regularly on publishing and intellectual property law and estate planning issues.

Tonya is a writer, performance poet, and the author of numerous books, including *Contracts Companion for Writers*, *Copyright Companion for Writers*, and *Literary Law Guide for Authors: Copyright, Trademark, and Contracts in Plain Language*, as well as two books of poetry, *Seasons of Her* and *SHINE!* Her short story, *Not Tonight*, appears in an anthology titled *Proverbs for the People*, published by Kensington.

Tonya attended Northwestern University on a four-year tennis scholarship, and thereafter she competed on the women's professional tennis circuit and played most notably in the US Open, Virginia Slims of Philadelphia, and Lipton in 1993. She then attended Howard University on an academic scholarship, served as editor-in-chief of the *Howard Law Journal*, and graduated with honors. She is a member of Alpha Kappa Alpha Sorority, Inc.

Tonya lives in Philadelphia with her husband, O. Russel Walls, III.

Literary Entrepreneur Series™ Information

Legal Write Publications publishes legal reference guides
with the rights of writers in mind!™

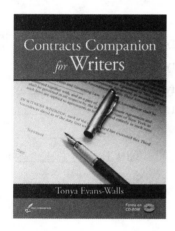

*Essential writer's reference on
how to make the best deals
"in writing"*

*A layperson's guide to the A to
Zs of copyright protection*

*An indispensable writing
tool for those who want
to understand the legal
advantages, disadvantages,
and intricacies involved in
the business of writing*

Price: $22.95

Price: $19.95

Price: $22.95

Category: Writing, Law, Reference
Pages: 160
Book Type: Paper
Size: 8 1/2 x 11
ISBN: 096745798X
ISBN13: 9780967457987

Category: Writing, Law, Reference
Pages: 160
Book Type: Paper
Size: 8 1/2 x 11
ISBN: 0967457998
ISBN13: 9780967457994

Category: Writing, Law, Reference
Pages: 208
Book Type: Paper
Size: 8 1/2 x 11
ISBN: 0967457971
ISBN13: 9780967457970

Publication and Ordering Information

For info: info@legalwritepublications.com

Web orders: www.legalwritepublications.com

Fax orders: (215) 438-0469. Copy and send this form.

Phone orders: (215) 438-0468. Have your credit card ready.

Mail orders: LWP Order Fulfillment, P.O. Box 25216, Philadelphia, PA, 19119. USA.

Bulk orders: Email or call for discounts and specials for
                     clubs, schools, and organizations.

Trade orders: Trade orders handled by Independent Publishers Group:

          Phone: (800) 888-4741

          Email/Web: orders@ipgbook.com   www.ipgbook.com

          Mail: Independent Publishers Group
                           Order Department
                           814 North Franklin Street
                           Chicago, IL 60610

❑ Contracts Companion for Writers   List $22.95   Quantity ___   Cost _____

❑ Copyright Companion for Writers   List $19.95   Quantity ___   Cost _____

❑ Literary Law Guide for Authors (2nd ed)   List $22.95   Quantity ___   Cost _____

❑ Literary Law Guide for Authors (1st ed.)   List $15.95   Quantity ___   Cost _____

                                           Subtotal _____

                                       Sales Tax _____

                                       Shipping _____

                                       TOTAL _____

Please send me information on *(check all that apply)*:

❑ Other books   ❑ Speaker Services   ❑ Seminars/Events/Performances   ❑ e-Newsletter

Name: _____

Address: _____

City: _____ State: _____ Zip: _____

Phone: _____ Email: _____

     • **Sales tax:** Please add 6% for products   • **Shipping:** $4.50 US for the first book, $2.00
       shipped to Pennsylvania addresses outside of   US for each additional book. US and Canada
       Philadelphia and 7% for Philadelphia addresses.   only. Call for Int'l orders.

Payment Method:

❑ Check/Money Order   ❑ Credit card *(circle one)*: Visa   MasterCard   Am Ex

Card number: _____ Exp: _____ Security Code: _____

Name on card: _____

Billing Address *(if different from above)*

Publication and Ordering Information

For info: info@legalwritepublications.com

Web orders: www.legalwritepublications.com

Fax orders: (215) 438-0469. Copy and send this form.

Phone orders: (215) 438-0468. Have your credit card ready.

Mail orders: LWP Order Fulfillment, P.O. Box 25216, Philadelphia, PA, 19119. USA.

Bulk orders: Email or call for discounts and specials for clubs, schools, and organizations.

Trade orders: Trade orders handled by Independent Publishers Group:

         Phone: (800) 888-4741

         Email/Web: orders@ipgbook.com   www.ipgbook.com

         Mail: Independent Publishers Group
                  Order Department
                  814 North Franklin Street
                  Chicago, IL 60610

❑ Contracts Companion for Writers   List $22.95   Quantity ___   Cost _____

❑ Copyright Companion for Writers   List $19.95   Quantity ___   Cost _____

❑ Literary Law Guide for Authors (2nd ed)   List $22.95   Quantity ___   Cost _____

❑ Literary Law Guide for Authors (1st ed.)   List $15.95   Quantity ___   Cost _____

                                        Subtotal _____

                                        Sales Tax _____

                                        Shipping _____

                                        TOTAL _____

Please send me information on *(check all that apply):*

❑ Other books   ❑ Speaker Services   ❑ Seminars/Events/Performances   ❑ e-Newsletter

Name: _____

Address: _____

City: _____ State: _____ Zip: _____

Phone: _____ Email: _____

- **Sales tax:** Please add 6% for products shipped to Pennsylvania addresses outside of Philadelphia and 7% for Philadelphia addresses.

- **Shipping:** $4.50 US for the first book, $2.00 US for each additional book. US and Canada only. Call for Int'l orders.

Payment Method:

❑ Check/Money Order   ❑ Credit card *(circle one)*: Visa   MasterCard   Am Ex

Card number: _____ Exp: _____ Security Code: _____

Name on card: _____

Billing Address *(if different from above)*